Flake | **Mảnh**

WRITER **DAN LEE**

CO-CREATOR **CHI NGUYEN**

CURRENCY PRESS
The performing arts publisher

RED STITCH

THE
ACTORS'
THEATRE

CURRENT THEATRE SERIES

First published in 2023
by Currency Press
Gadigal Land, PO Box 2287 Strawberry Hills, NSW, 2012, Australia
enquiries@currency.com.au
www.currency.com.au

in association with Red Stitch

Typeset by Brighton Gray for Currency Press.
Cover image by Robert Blackburn.
Front cover shows Robert Menzies, Joe Petruzzi and Phoebe Phuoc Nguyen.
Cover design by Emma Bennetts.

Currency Press acknowledges the Traditional Owners of the Country on which we live and work. We pay our respects to all Aboriginal and Torres Strait Islander Elders, past and present.

A catalogue record for this book is available from the National Library of Australia

Contents

Flake was first produced by Red Stitch Actors' Theatre at the Red Stitch Theatre, St Kilda, on the lands of the Boon Wurrung and Wurundjeri Woi Wurrung peoples of the Kulin Nation, on 11 October 2023, with the following cast:

BOB	Robert Menzies
MURPH	Joe Petruzzi
DUYÊN	Phoebe Phuoc Nguyen

Director, Ella Caldwell
Set and Costume Design, Jacob Battista
Lighting Designer, Jason Ng Junjie
Composition and Sound Designer, Daniel Nixon
Set Design Associate / Scenic Painter, Khue Nguyen
Dialect Coach, Yuanlei (Nikki) Zhao
Dramaturg, Tom Healey
Stage Manager, Finn McLeish
Assistant Stage Manager, Finleigh Wadsworth

CHARACTERS

BOB, Australian baby boomer
MURPH, Australian baby boomer
DUYÊN, Vietnamese woman, mid-20s

SETTING

The whole play takes place in a small, cluttered kitchen, in a
house, on the outskirts of Hanoi, Vietnam. There is a dining table
and chairs, a fridge, a sink, kitchenette area with camp style
portable gas cooker and a large Bonsai tree. There's a window
onto the narrow lane outside and stairs going up to the four floors
above. The kitchen is on the ground floor with the garage where
the motor bikes are parked at night.

NOTES

A dash (—) indicates an interruption of speech or train of thought.

An ellipsis (…) indicates either a trailing off, a new thought
emerging or a searching for the words.

A slash (/) indicates where the next line overlaps.

This play text went to press before the end of rehearsals and may
differ from the play as performed.

1

*A Hanoi kitchen in darkness. A small motorbike is heard approaching.
The headlight streams through the window and passes across the inside
of the kitchen giving us a brief preview of the world of the play. It stops
and shines out at the audience for a moment. The engine stops and the
headlight is shut off and the stage is in darkness again.*

*A man fumbles his way into the house in the dark and searches for the
light switch. He finds the fridge instead, which is full of beer and casts
a light across the room as he opens the door. He takes out two cans
before shutting it again. He rummages along the wall, still looking for
the light, bangs into the bench, grunts and drops one of the cans on the
floor. He curses and abandons the search for the light, leans against
the sink. For a moment nothing happens and all is silent. The man in
the dark is* MURPH.

He opens a can which explodes all over him.

MURPH: Faaaakenell!

> DUYÊN *enters and immediately turns on the light. She knows where
> it is.* MURPH *is revealed, like a flash photo of a nocturnal animal—
> contrived and caricatured—up against the sink, cowering beneath
> the naked bulb that swings directly above his head. He's wearing
> a loose, wet, faded Hawaiian shirt and a baseball cap plastic
> helmet, that is sitting high and awkward on his head. He shrieks
> dramatically.* DUYÊN *recoils in horror—which is what he was
> hoping for and makes him laugh hysterically.*

> MURPH *notices that he is covered in beer and abruptly stops
> laughing.*

Aaah shit!

> *He grabs a nearby tea towel and tries, without much success, to
> dry himself.*

> DUYÊN *looks around the room. She notices the Bonsai tree and
> walks straight over to it.*

DUYÊN: Where did you get this?

MURPH: It was here when he moved in, I think. The tree, the table—it's not like he brought anything with him.

He watches her for a while as she examines the tree.

Ah … excuse me.

She looks around the room—really taking it all in as if she's trying to jog her memory.

'Excuse me, miss.'

She snaps out of it, walks over to him. Looks at his wet shirt and grabs the unopened beer from him.

DUYÊN: I'll have that one then.

She opens the beer.

How long have you lived here?

MURPH: I don't— Please, have a seat.

DUYÊN *sits at the table, drinks her beer and waits for more information.*

Bob lives here.

MURPH *gets another beer from the fridge. He sits down and casually takes a cigarette out of the packet in his top pocket. He points the packet in* DUYÊN*'s direction.*

I'm just visiting.

She shakes her head. He lights the cigarette and coughs immediately. He tries, unsuccessfully, to suppress a coughing fit with his hand over his mouth.

I do … I do beg … I do beg your pardon …

He coughs again—worse than the first time. He's really hacking up a lung now. DUYÊN *is unmoved. He manages to get it under control.*

Sorry, it's these cheap darts. 'Asbestos and DDT flavour!'
I'm not usually this—

DUYÊN: Drunk?

MURPH: I was going to say clumsy, actually.

DUYÊN: Who was the guy in the *Mission Impossible* T-shirt?

MURPH: That was my tour guide … Taxi driver slash tour guide slash … whatever you need. Drove me round all day, stopping every half-hour to lean up against a temple and smoke these fucking darts— What say we ease up on the temples! I said. Temples on top of temples—inside temples. What is it with Asia and temples?

DUYÊN: What is it with Europe and churches?

MURPH *smiles—touché.*

He was up to no good.

MURPH: Who was?

DUYÊN: The man with the … impossible mission.

MURPH *is confused.*

Your 'tour guide'.

MURPH *chuckles with acknowledgement.*

MURPH: Didn't speak a word of English, you know. Didn't matter though. Most communication is non-verbal.

See, most people just learn a couple of clunky phrases and then totally disconnect from their bodies. They just stand there aggressively repeating themselves at increasing volume. Whereas …

He closes his eyes, breathes in deeply and exhales slowly. Opens his eyes.

I let expression flow from my whole body.

DUYÊN *laughs heartily.*

The look on MURPH*'s face tells her that he was not trying to be funny.*

After a brief pause.

DUYÊN: So, you, sort of … dance, your way around the world, like a … jolly jester.

Short pause.

Little hat with bells on the ends.

MURPH: She's taking the piss out of me … And yet, here. She. Is.

DUYÊN: I couldn't leave you there in the street.

MURPH: An act of charity.

DUYÊN: I would have felt terrible if something had happened to you.

MURPH: You would never have known if something terrible had happened to me unless …

DUYÊN: Unless?

MURPH: Unless you intended to see me again.

DUYÊN: You really do come up with some extraordinary stories, don't you?

MURPH: A good story is universal. It wraps the general in the particular while remaining somehow familiar enough to transcend different cultures and languages.

> MURPH *starts moving his head from side to side and pursing his lips—trying to enact Charlie Chaplin or Buster Keaton but doing it so badly that neither* DUYÊN *or the audience can pick it.*

DUYÊN: Oh dear. What are we doing now?

> *He stands up and starts doing the Chaplin waddle with the cane.* DUYÊN *starts laughing—*MURPH *is in his element.*

MURPH: Whatsisname, proved it years ago!

DUYÊN: Did he?

MURPH: And the other one!

DUYÊN: Whatshisname and the other one—what a pair!

> MURPH *stops for a second. Takes a deep breath and starts again.*

Do you mean … Charlie Chaplin?

MURPH: That's it! Charlie Chaplin and Buster Keaton—totally silent and yet accessible to everyone.

> MURPH *sits down again.*

> *Pause.*

DUYÊN: I haven't the slightest idea what we're talking about.

MURPH: The golden age of physical comedy.

> DUYÊN *looks unconvinced—*MURPH *searches for the point.*

Taxi drivers!

DUYÊN: With sinister intentions.

MURPH: That's it!

DUYÊN: Not totally seeing the connection but …

MURPH: Soon as you resort to language you've given in to over-simplification.

DUYÊN: Not in your case.

MURPH: What?

DUYÊN: And I assumed you were just old and drunk.

MURPH: I am not old!

Beat.

Age is just candles on a cake!

DUYÊN: True. And old age is just running out of room!

Short pause.

On the cake.

MURPH: Ah, tongue-in-cheek. Well, I think you'll get on well with Bob.

DUYÊN: Does he speak English?

MURPH: And French.

DUYÊN: Really?

MURPH: Vietnamese!

DUYÊN: He speaks Vietnamese?

MURPH: Sure does.

DUYÊN: Well, that's … that's, I mean, Vietnamese is hard—

MURPH: Xin Chao! Cam on! He taught me those—the taxi driver, I mean.

Awkward pause.

The point is; a good bloke's a good bloke. I'm a good bloke. Obviously. So, I know a good bloke when I see one.

DUYÊN: He was going to drive you up a dark lane and take your wallet.

MURPH: Nonsense!

DUYÊN: Look at you!

MURPH: I'm a gregarious man of adventure!

DUYÊN: You're a shit-faced 'man of adventure'.

MURPH: I've got drunk with taxi drivers all over the world! A cabbie in Rio once took me to a huge party on the beach. I was his last fare for the night and I just remember his eyes in the mirror—a certain twinkle and I knew an adventure had begun. We scrambled over a sand dune and there it was—like a blazing carnival. This utterly … cinematic—Latin—fire-twirling—dance party on the beach. Bonfires and tequila! We danced great trenches in the sand! Communicating authentically— Athletically! Shaking off the bondage of language like the clothes on our backs. Free—FREE! Beneath the full moon!

> DUYÊN *delivers a little light applause.*

Woke up on the sand the next morning. Waves crashing all around.

DUYÊN: Nostalgia for your youth.

MURPH: This was last year!

> DUYÊN *laughs.*

You gotta go to Rio—I'll take you. I'll take you now, Goddamnit! What time is it?

> DUYÊN *looks at her watch.*

DUYÊN: Oh shit! It's two o'clock.

> MURPH *gets up and starts looking for something to play music on.*

MURPH: Please. Don't go!

DUYÊN: I really / have to—

> MURPH *sings the first verse of 'Baby, Please Don't Go' by Van Morrison and Them.*

> MURPH *sings the guitar solo that follows as he searches for and eventually finds the radio.*

MURPH: Aha!

> *He turns on the radio. There is some Vietnamese music playing.*

We haven't had a chance to communicate authentically yet.

> *He raises an eyebrow.*

DUYÊN: And that's my cue to leave.

> *She heads for the door.*

Thanks for the beer and you know.

> *He intercepts her as she passes him. Sweeps her up in a caricatured Latin dance move and starts dancing.*

> *She's not a dancer but she is somewhat relieved that dancing is his intention. She humours him for a moment or two. Then she attempts to leave again.*

MURPH: John McCain!

The presidential candidate.

You asked me how I acquired my tour guide— Well! We were driving across Chook Back Lake—

DUYÊN: Truc Bach—

MURPH: Exactly! … The taxi driver wasn't saying much. So, I shouted—John McCain!

The plane in the lake? You can see the landing gear sticking out of the water!

He was shot down in sixty-eight. Ejected. Parachuted—had a nice long stay in the Hanoi Hilton.

I love that they left it there sticking out of the lake. It's like a … scarecrow.

Surely you know about the plane in the lake?

I just blurted it out—John McCain! Pointing at the lake. He thought that was fucking brilliant. I mean he really came to life— laughing and slapping the steering wheel. We both laughed and shouted John McCain and pointed at the lake. That's all it takes, see. A little bit of local knowledge is all you need to make an authentic connection.

He starts dancing again and wants her to join him.

DUYÊN: What do you mean, a scarecrow?

MURPH: A strawman standing in a cornfield with a wooden stake up his ass.

BOB *slowly starts coming down the stairs, unseen by both of them. He stops and watches.*

MURPH *starts dancing like the Scarecrow from* The Wizard of Oz.

DUYÊN: I know what a scarecrow is! Why is the plane a scarecrow?

MURPH: [*still doing his scarecrow impression*] It's a warning. It says: This is what happens when you fly over Hanoi with malicious intent.

He sings the first line of the Scarecrow's song. BOB *appears in the kitchen behind them.*

BOB: [*singing*] If he only had a brain!

MURPH: Fuck me!

BOB: Ông ta đang bắt chước thằng bù nhìn trong truyện *Wizard of Oz*. Cô biết nó không? (He's copying the scarecrow character from *The Wizard of Oz*. You know it?)

DUYÊN: Dạ không. (No.)

BOB: Thằng bù nhìn không có óc, rất giống ông ta. (The Scarecrow has no brain, much like him.)

[*To* MURPH] I told her that the scarecrow has no brain so the impression comes naturally to you.

MURPH: She speaks English better than me.

This is the famous Bob. Bob this is … this is … a girl I met in a bar somewhere.

DUYÊN: Duyên.

MURPH: Sorry.

BOB: Hello, Duyên.

MURPH: She kindly offered to give me a lift home on her motorbike.

BOB: You offered?

DUYÊN: Insisted.

BOB: And you managed to get her in the house.

[*To* DUYÊN] Surely you can see, he's up to no good.

DUYÊN: Do you think he'll try to steal my wallet?

BOB: Just your youth.

MURPH: I did warn you about him.

BOB *gets a beer out of the fridge.*

BOB: Why would you do that?

MURPH: I wanted her to be prepared.

BOB *sits down at the table opposite* MURPH*, opens his beer and proceeds to light a cigarette.*

DUYÊN: He gave a fairly unflattering description of you.

BOB: Did he?

MURPH: … You don't always play well with others.

BOB: Well, I don't like people, if that's what you mean.

DUYÊN: He said you were like an old rescue dog.

MURPH: Like! I said you were, a bit 'like' a rescue dog because they're often really gentle and timid but you know—sometimes … out of nowhere …

DUYÊN: They maul the children.

MURPH: Exactly! But apart from that …
DUYÊN: Yeah, apart from that …

> BOB *just stares at* MURPH *in silence.* MURPH *gestures at* BOB.

MURPH: You see … Zooanne—
DUYÊN: Duyên.
MURPH: Zoo …
DUYÊN: Du-yên.
MURPH: … Zoo Anne, so much communication is non-verbal. The body tells us everything we need to know, gestures, facial expressions—

> BOB *suddenly snaps out of it, lunges across the table and grabs* MURPH *by the shirt front. He pulls him into the centre of the table. Their faces are very close together.* BOB *has a cigarette in his teeth.* MURPH *is trying to avoid the smoke. He holds him there a while without saying anything. Then lets him go and they both fall back into their seats.* BOB *takes the cigarette from his mouth and takes a casual swig on his beer.*

BOB: Pick up anything useful from that?

> *Tense pause … then* BOB *contrives a smile. Everyone relaxes.*

MURPH: … I've just been telling her about John McCain in the lake.
BOB: Từ đấy, những ông Tây già cứ rơi từ trên trời xuống!
MURPH: Righto, what are you saying?
BOB: I said old white men have been dropping out of the sky ever since.
DUYÊN: Yep. That's what he said.
BOB: The white ghosts of Asia—floating through the countryside— haunting young women—
MURPH: What's that prison called Bob?
BOB: The Hanoi Hilton. He must have had some conflicting emotions—
MURPH: No. No—
BOB: I mean, he's just been bombing them for fuck's sake! A few tense moments, no doubt, as the parachute opened and he floated down to earth. But the decent, hard-working folks of Hanoi managed to restrain their reasonably homicidal urges and instead they drag him off to … to …

> *Pause.*

Wait!

Long angry pause.

Hoa Lo! That's it! I just woke up! What do you want from me?

    They dragged him off to Hoa Lo prison, where he spent the rest of the war playing ping pong and perfecting his needlepoint—now he's a Sepo fucking hero.

    Ông ấy điên diên nhưng vô hại. Cái nón hợp với ông ấy nhỉ? (He seems crazy but he's harmless. The hat suits him don't you think?)

DUYÊN: Vâng. Vâng. (Yes. Yes.)

BOB: Ông ấy uống nhiều lắm phải không? (He drank a lot right?)

DUYÊN: Rất chuyên nghiệp. (Like a professional.)

BOB: Ông ấy có hát không? (Did he start to sing?)

DUYÊN: Không ai nghe nên không sao. (No-one listened so it's alright.)

    Suddenly the music changes—K-Pop, with a good beat.

    MURPH *sweeps in and grabs* DUYÊN *again. They dance around and laugh.* BOB *watches and drinks.*

MURPH: I like this! Is this Vietnamese music?

DUYÊN: I don't think so.

BOB: K-Pop.

MURPH: What?

BOB: K-Pop!

DUYÊN: Korean Pop!

MURPH: Is it?

BOB: The kids love it— Fuck knows why.

MURPH: It's fantastic!

BOB: Yeah—He's an old K-Popper from way back.

    Ông ấy cứ giật giật như vậy, thận sẽ nổ ra đường đít mất! (If he keeps thrashing around like that, his kidney will pop out of his ass!)

    DUYÊN *laughs.*

MURPH: What did he say?

DUYÊN: K-Pop! As in … Kidney?

MURPH: What?

DUYÊN: Might be the first time that sentence has ever been said in Vietnamese.

BOB: Giật giật. Nổ nổ! (Thrashy thrashy. Poppy poppy!)

    They laugh.

MURPH: Can you speak English please!

BOB: Just explaining the distressing palsy you call dancing.

He points at MURPH's *dancing.*

Can be quite a shock to a girl when it first happens.

MURPH *tries to get* BOB *up to dance.*

Nothing a good neurosurgeon couldn't fix with the quick flick of the wrist!

MURPH *tries again,* BOB *resists.*

Don't be alarmed. It'll pass soon enough.

MURPH *reaches out—*BOB *pulls away aggressively.*

STOP IT! I DON'T WANT TO FUCKING DANCE, ALRIGHT!
When have I ever wanted to fucking dance?
Just keep it to yourself!

Pause.

MURPH: Righto—

DUYÊN: I'd better go—

BOB: What exactly is it about my demeanour that indicates to you that I'd be up for a bit of disco dancing?!

Pause.

MURPH *keeps dancing uncomfortably for a bit before stopping. The music plays. None of them move except* BOB *smoking.*

MURPH: Okay! Well …

BOB: Well, what!

MURPH: Fuck a duck, Bob! You're a moody bastard these days.

BOB *gets up and walks toward the stairs.*

DUYÊN: [*to* MURPH] Fuck a duck?

MURPH *rolls his eyes.*

BOB *stops and stares at the ground in front of him for a moment.*

BOB: Zack—

Beat.

He looks up and around the room until he notices them standing there. He tries to mask his surprise at seeing them.

MURPH: You right, mate?

BOB: Just keep it down!

He quickly looks away and starts walking up the stairs.

DUYÊN: Hey Bob!

He stops and turns back.

This tree—where did you get it from?

BOB: It was a gift from the landlady.

DUYÊN: A gift?

BOB: She was under the impression it would ease my loneliness.

BOB *goes up into his bedroom.*

MURPH: He better rest. He's taking me to Ha Long Bay tomorrow and then Sapa after that.

DUYÊN: Who's Zack?

MURPH: His son in Australia.

DUYÊN: Is he okay?

MURPH: He made himself lunch the other day and tipped it straight into the bin. He wouldn't have noticed at all if I hadn't pointed it out.

DUYÊN: How long has he been here?

MURPH: Maybe … fifteen years.

DUYÊN: But. I mean … has he been in this house the whole time?

MURPH: Da Nang first. Maybe ten years here and Da Nang before that.

DUYÊN: Oh. So, he's living here. Like permanently.

MURPH: As permanent as permanent gets for Bob. Says he's not going back to Australia.

DUYÊN: Is he the same age as you?

MURPH: Exactly— We've known each other forever.

DUYÊN: Has he got a doctor here? Just, given his age and being here permanently—might be a good idea.

DUYÊN *is looking past* MURPH *to the tree. She walks across to take another look at the pot. She squats down to look at the pot. She turns it slightly and reads, out loud, a name that has been stamped into the ceramic.*

Huỳnh Phú Vinh …

> MURPH *goes over to the stairs again and peers up toward Bob's bedroom.*

MURPH: What's that?

BOB: Sometimes when people make pots, they stamp their name into them.

MURPH: Just a sec …

> MURPH *quickly and quietly tiptoes up the stairs to check that Bob has really gone to bed.*

> *She turns the pot a little more and a plastic bag drops out on the table. She turns quickly to check if Murph is still there. Seeing that he isn't, she keeps talking while she examines the dose. The bag contains a syringe and a couple of small glass ampules.*

DUYÊN: Across the road there, through the—you know—the cumquat field—not far—is the Red River. Good—

> *She puts the bag back under the pot and gets up.*

… very good clay. For ceramic pots …

> *She backs quietly away from the table.*

People just dig it straight out of the—the riverbank…

> *She makes a hasty exit.*

> MURPH *comes back down.*

MURPH: Just wanted to make sure bugalugs…

> MURPH *sees that she has gone. He hears the motorbike start up and he runs to the window, shouting after her.*

Wait!

> *She takes off up the lane.*

2

The same Hanoi kitchen. BOB *and* MURPH *have just returned from their trip to Ha Long Bay.*

BOB *enters. He waters the Bonsai. He goes to the cupboard. He pulls out a bottle of whisky, takes two glasses and goes back to the table. He pours two drinks, waits, looks around, expecting someone. He quickly drinks one and then refills it, drinks it again and refills it again just as a toilet flush is heard from upstairs.*

BOB *quickly sits down and observes the tree.*

MURPH *comes out of the bathroom at the top of the stairs wiping his wet hands on his jeans.*

MURPH: Three days, all up. Maybe four.

> *Murph's mobile phone interrupts; bleats out an incoming message. He pulls the phone out of his shirt pocket and reads the message. He tries to talk while reading.*

It might have been … it might have been four actually … still. You know. They can just ah … they can …

> *He replies to the text.*

They make a … a … they ah … sorry. Just give me a sec.

BOB: I see you're a digital native.

> MURPH *raises his hand—trying to concentrate.*

About as native as a cane toad …

> MURPH *ignores him this time.*

You're the cane toad of the digital world!

> MURPH *looks up and stares forward intensely.*

The face of catastrophic multitasking failure, right there, folks.

MURPH: Shut up, will you!

> MURPH *starts jabbing the phone with his index finger.*

BOB: The old hunt-and-peck method.

MURPH: What!

BOB: In your own time.

MURPH: Jesus Christ you're like a toddler.

BOB: Don't forget to breathe.

MURPH: Just give us a tick, will ya?

BOB: Carry on, Steve Jobs.

> MURPH *finishes the text message.*

MURPH: Yeah. So, where was I? … That's right!

> They—they make a couple of incisions, send in a robot with a scalpel and a microscope.

BOB: Who are we talking about?

MURPH: You remember Mick.

> We used to go to his grandmother's place in Williamstown to buy grass … when Tom and Zack were babies.

BOB: His grandmother?

MURPH: Yeah. His— You don't remember? He was dealing out of the shed— Did some time for it actually; during that … Fraser era, crackdown— Seventy-five or … Bastard wanted to make a point— started giving first offenders custodials. Fucking ridiculous really. Knackered his job prospects … no? He needed an inconspicuous place to operate out of and his gran was delighted to have him round more often. It was the perfect cover; the old girl gardening in the front yard all day. Tire swans. Garden gnomes and flowers. Got busted carrying a couple of plants on the back seat of the EH.

> You really don't remember?

> MURPH *sits down next to* BOB *and they both observe the bonsai.*

Neville's twenty-first! He was the one wearing the gorilla suit.

BOB: Jesus Christ! Niftie's twenty-first.

MURPH: Mick was always wearing that fucking thing—those parties on the beach. Sandringham and ah … Black Rock.

BOB: Yes! I remember those parties.

> *Beat.*

MURPH: So yeah, just two small incisions, they're in, they're out, couple of stitches and he drove himself home on the third day—or the … or the fourth.

BOB: Quick as you like.

MURPH: No more cracking you open like a fucking oyster.

BOB: No zipper then?

MURPH: Nah. Just … nah he looked, all right. I mean, he looked tired—
he was on a lot of medication.

BOB: But he was more or less.

MURPH: Yeah. Back to normal. More or less.

BOB: With certain … limitations.

MURPH: Well yeah but that's up to the individual. There's certain—
There's more … they don't advise certain stuff. You know.

BOB: And the funnelling begins.

MURPH: What do you mean?

BOB: The great narrowing … a little flutter, a dizzy spell, an
imperceptible narrowing of the arteries and then the rest of your life
is a series doctors advising you against things.

MURPH: There's all sorts of amazing shit they can do nowadays. Non-
invasive surgeries.

  BOB *laughs*

What?

BOB: Non-invasive surgery!

  Hopelessly optimistic? No? Assisted suicide?

MURPH: What the fuck are you talking about?

BOB: Oh! That reminds me!

MURPH: Anyway, he dropped dead on the fucking bus two weeks later.

BOB: What?

  Hang on … He's dead?

MURPH: Yeah. That's what I've been telling you for the last / half-hour!

BOB: Just like that? Commuting?

MURPH: Anything could happen. And it could happen at any moment.

  Long pause.

BOB: What?

MURPH: And he's back.

  BOB *suddenly raises his glass.*

BOB: To Mick!

  MURPH *raises his glass.*

MURPH: Mick.

BOB *gets a couple more beers from the fridge.*

BOB: My neck is knackered from that bed.

MURPH: I don't think we were on the right boat, you know. The one in the brochure—did we book the—was it the deluxe or—'cause that looked like the one in the other photo—on the other ah …

BOB: Ignore the photos!

MURPH: Righto!

BOB: The photos are purely decorative. You learn that very early on …

Beat.

Right! Sapa next. 'Beautiful mountain village to take special lady.' Alternatively: 'Geriatric halfwit with a penchant for teenage virgins.'

MURPH: Fuck off.

BOB: I prefer Sapa to Ha Long Bay actually, not quite the same level of mayhem.

MURPH: Ha Long Bay was like a cattle market.

BOB: Bewildered cattle gathering outside the abattoir.

MURPH: Never seen so many bumbags and knee-high socks.

BOB: Fucking tourists!

MURPH: Heads on 'em like mice.

Beat.

Thought that old couple weren't going to get on the boat for a second there. The poor old duck in the hat, you know—she was holding on—she was looking green around the gills before we even left the dock.

BOB: You know they were the same age as us, right?

MURPH: I don't think so.

BOB: How old would you say they were?

MURPH: … Seventy-five at least. Eighty.

BOB: Seventy-one. I saw their passports, he was seventy-one, she was seventy.

MURPH: How did you / see—

BOB: How old are you?

MURPH: Same age as you.

BOB: Yeah, so how old are you?

MURPH: What?

BOB: How old are you?

MURPH: Almost sixty-nine.

What?

What!

BOB: They are us! Don't you see? We are them and they are us. We're interchangeable—just two more bovine boomers queuing up to be … processed.

MURPH: We had a conspicuous lack of bumbags though.

Pause.

BOB: I'm an old man, Murph.

MURPH: Ay?

BOB: You know it's going to happen in theory, but you don't for a second imagine that it actually will.

MURPH: What does that mean?

BOB: I was shaving the other day.

MURPH: Right …

BOB: I was having a shave and I got a momentary glimpse of the truth—a real 'Naked Lunch' moment. Everything else disappeared and there. I. Was.

MURPH: Fuck.

BOB: Look at my hands.

MURPH: Ay?

BOB: Look at my hands.

MURPH: What about them?

BOB: I'm an old man.

MURPH: You're fucking repeating yourself like / one!

BOB: Just another old white man floating around Asia like a fucking ghost.

MURPH: You're not that old.

BOB: Yes, I am. And so are you!

MURPH: Don't bring me / into this.

BOB: If I'm an old— No! … If I'm an old man then you are too.

BOB *stands up.*

Look at me … Look at me!

MURPH: Yeah all / right.

BOB: I'm an old man, aren't I?

MURPH: If you say so.

BOB: We both are.

MURPH: I'm not.

BOB: You are!

MURPH: Will you just—I told you—you just—fuck / man!

BOB: You! … Are an old / man—

MURPH: Don't start / doing this thing—this—

BOB: No. No. Wait! Wait—I saw you walking down the lane when you first arrived and you looked like you'd escaped from somewhere— wandered off—got lost … in a Hawaiian shirt.

MURPH: Sixty-eight's not old!

BOB: Look at that poor old fella! I said to myself.

MURPH: Righto!

BOB: That poor ole fella— Oh shit! It's Murph!

    Backpack— Rolly cigarettes— Long hair. Look at ya!

MURPH: Yeah. Yeah.

BOB: Poor old bastard, I thought.

MURPH: Righto, righto!

BOB: You know I'm half an inch shorter?

MURPH: Is that a fact?

BOB: Murph …

    Murph!

MURPH: What?

> BOB *looks at him over his glasses.*

Geeet fucked!

> BOB *just keeps staring at him.*

You might be but I'm / not.

BOB: I want to hear you say it.

> MURPH *dismisses him.*

Take off your shirt.

MURPH: What?

BOB: Take your shirt off.

MURPH: You pissed already?

BOB: Just shut up and take off your shirt …

> *They wait.*

Didn't think so. You know why?

MURPH: I'm not / going to give—I'm not—I'm not going to.

BOB: 'Cause you're an old man! You're an old man and you fucking look like one— Saggy tits—chest hair like rusty wire splattered with birdshit. We're starting to look mummified … translucent!

> BOB *takes off his shirt.*

MURPH: Jesus Christ!

BOB: This isn't me! At some point I stopped being me and started being this.

MURPH: For fuck's sake!

> BOB *puts his shirt back on and sits down again.*

BOB: You think she didn't notice?

MURPH: Who?

BOB: The girl.

MURPH: What girl?

BOB: Here! The other night! You were giving her the old moves but by Christ it was a savage uphill pedal wasn't it.

MURPH: Women don't care about that sort of thing.

BOB: Maybe not here.

MURPH: What do you mean by that?

BOB: You know exactly what I mean by that— She fucking noticed, mate. She just can't afford to care.

> *Pause.*

So, rather than join you, flapping about in the kiddie pool of old-age denial, I have cast aside the Hawaiian print floaties and the pool safe nappies in favour of a good old-fashioned exit strategy.

MURPH: Might need to unpack that a bit.

BOB: I got a dose! You know, a lethal shot.

> *A rat runs along the kitchen bench.*

> MURPH *screams and jumps up!*

MURPH: It's gone behind the fridge!

> BOB *leaps up.*

BOB: Get out of there ya bastard! The other morning—

> *Murphs's phone receives another message.*

I came down and he was standing in the middle of the room looking at me. Unperturbed! 'I'm not frightened of you, old man!'

MURPH *reads the message while* BOB *starts banging around behind the fridge with a broomstick.*

Then—the creepiest thing—you listening?

MURPH *looks up at* BOB.

The bastard *walked* away—didn't run! Walked. Casually! Strolled! Sauntered across the room like a belligerent teenager. I'm telling you, when the rodents start skulking off to their room, it's a fucking sign … a sign of …

MURPH: Being baited.

BOB: What?

He puts the phone away again.

MURPH: They get slow like that when they've taken a bait.

Beat.

BOB: The bastard's biding his time. Planning his ascent!

Get out of there ya big bastard! You, don't intimidate me!

Morphine mate! I thought I'd end up with heroin but this is better, pharmaceutical predictability in terms of, you know, strength and it's a liquid—so it's ready to go … we were talking about it, last time I saw you.

MURPH: You're a fucking laugh riot today.

Another message.

BOB: Who the fuck is that?

MURPH *reads.*

MURPH: Hang on.

Replies as quickly as possible. Puts it away and looks at BOB.

Right.

Go!

BOB: I was just telling you. I've got it sorted. So, you know, when the time comes— Hey pass us a smoke, will you?

MURPH: You're not really going to do that.

BOB *lights a cigarette.*

BOB: I fucking will.

MURPH: No, you won't.

BOB: You wanna bet on it?

MURPH: You'll fuck it up.

BOB: How hard can it be? I had to put the toilet seat back on the other day—YouTube—piece of piss.

MURPH: You're kidding.

BOB: Some teenager in Idaho will walk me through it.

Failing that … I'll get Zack to take care of it! When he notices piss stains on my trousers and I can't light a cigarette any more.

MURPH: When was the last time you spoke to Zack, by the way?

Bob! Forget about the fucking rat and tell me how long it's been since you spoke to Zack …

BOB *abandons the rat hunt.*

BOB: I got it off the bride's brother.

MURPH: You what?

BOB: The dose!

MURPH: Forget the dose for a / minute!

BOB: There was one of those big noisy weddings in the lane a few months back and the young bloke took me into town, he had some rough mates, I was joking about it and then bang there it was. You just have to mention it, right?

MURPH: … You told them what you wanted it for?

BOB: Of course, I was trying to describe the old maximum-security departure lounges back in Oz.

MURPH: The what?

BOB: You know the fucking nursing homes. They didn't know what I was talking about, of course. Old people here live with their families. They all stay together—no nursing homes! They don't get left to drool away their final years in front of a TV with the sound turned down—I'm sure they would if they could afford to but, you know. One day they just drop off the perch. Roll their last rice-paper roll and …

MURPH: My oldest won't even let me stay the night at his place.

BOB: After everything we fought for. After the revolution, the social upheaval and reform. We changed the fucking world! And what do we get for it? A lethal dose. That's all we've got.

MURPH: Well, it's not all we've got.

BOB: I tell you what though, I feel better just knowing it's there.

MURPH: Yeah, but when do you take it?

BOB: Well, that's the million-dollar question, isn't it?

Some kind of self-administered … questionnaire, I suppose.

MURPH: You get less than fifteen out of twenty and …

BOB: The problem is: if you're too compos you won't want to do it and if you're too far gone you won't have the capacity to pull the pin, as it were. It's a fucking tight rope any way you look at it but, you know, with these medical advances you're so excited about, the bastards'll be keeping us alive even longer. No-one's allowed to fucking die anymore. But I tell you what Murph. I'm not going out the same way as Mum and Dad.

MURPH: You've gotta have a good relationship with your kids.

BOB *laughs.*

What?

BOB: Nothing Murph. You're right. You're absolutely right, my friend. My dear old friend.

Pause, drink, smoke. BOB *walks to the Bonsai, rotating the pot, inspecting from different angles.*

MURPH: Didn't think you'd have the patience for that?

BOB: I don't—I was thinking of pruning that branch there.

MURPH *gets up and takes a closer look at the Bonsai.*

The one shooting out from the base! It's ridiculous—look at it! So ridiculous, in fact, that I started thinking it must be there for a reason.

MURPH *strokes his chin. Views it from different angles. Nods to himself.*

What are you doing?

MURPH: What do you mean?

BOB: Ah, save it for your bimbos!

MURPH: What?

BOB: The impression of complex intellectual reasoning. It's classic Murph! Ah, don't get upset.

MURPH: I'm not upset.

BOB: Don't listen to me. I'm a cunt. I am! You know I am …

> *Pause.*

'Let me just take a moment to consider the myriad possibilities available to me as a result of my extensive experience in the field.' But you and I both know there's nothing going on up there … Ah, what a treat it is to see you again Murphias!

> *Pause.*

Come on mate! Don't fucking sook about it. You can't claim you weren't pretending. What do you expect!

> *Short pause.*

I hate the fucking thing anyway. It's so … deliberate—so loaded up with other people's intentions—I'm just the most recent in a long line of sad old bastards who've sat here gazing at it. Surely, they've all had some fucking plan for it, some … vision. And it just sits there bristling with stillness! Serenity masking the urgency of other peoples ideas— Disguising the corruption of nature— Look at it! Sitting there like an abandoned bag in an airport.

MURPH: Yeah … I'd try not to think of it like that.

BOB: Even the most benign things turn out to be explosive devices in the end.

MURPH: Jesus Christ Almighty.

BOB: Fuck it! Must be time to unleash the black death.

> BOB *gets up and opens the cupboard beneath the sink.*

I've been waiting for the right moment to bring this out.

> BOB *drags out a huge glass jar with muslin draped over it.*

I give you the secret to Hanoi's success!

> BOB *whips off the muslin revealing a huge glass jar filled with dark liquid, stringy matter suspended in it above a sediment of putrefied black rice.* BOB *takes out the ladle and fills two small ceramic cups.* MURPH *takes a sip. Then another. He considers the taste.*

Am I right?

> MURPH *takes another sip, further consideration.*

MURPH: Utter fucking bile.

BOB: Deceptively so.

MURPH: Notes of … raw sewerage?

BOB: It's an acquired taste.

> MURPH *sips and dry-retches.*

Ooops! That's quite normal.

> *Beat.*

See those strands of decaying mater?

MURPH: Not if I avert my eyes.

BOB: That's the source of its healing properties.

> *Murph's phone bleats out another message. He doesn't check it. It bleats again and again he doesn't check it.*

Well check it then.

> Is that your xe ôm guy?

MURPH: Nah, it can wait.

BOB: Who is it?

> MURPH *puts his phone away.*

Un. Believable.

MURPH: What?

> What?

BOB: That's her, isn't it? Fucking hell Murph. You're unstoppable. You're an old man and she's younger than your daughter!

> You're going to end up with children on every continent!

> *Beat.*

That's like old Gerry fucking Emma.

MURPH: Jesus Christ, Bob! Who's 'old' Gerry!

BOB: Does it matter? Old Gerry with the camera and the … the vomiting wife, you know.

MURPH: Why would you say something like that? Why do you say things like that? I mean you don't have to say things like that!

BOB: It's about the same age difference.

MURPH: Okay but, you don't—and you always load it up with …

BOB: The facts!

MURPH: You don't even know who I'm talking to!

BOB: True.

BOB *pours another glass of the black death.*

Bloody gorgeous though. You'd be a fool not to try it on.
Give her one for me, muscles!

He lifts his glass.

Cheers!
You're not drinking!

MURPH: I don't think I can. It's brutal.

BOB *stands up and declares loudly.*

BOB: This is the heart and soul of Hanoi! This horrible shit's been handed down for generations! It reaches back in time to the battlements of Huế! To the old Ly Dynasty when Hanoi was still Thang Long—the rising dragon.

BOB *gets two beers. Hands one to* MURPH.

MURPH: Fuck me!

BOB *smashes his can up against the one in* MURPH*'s hand.*

BOB: Tell me something, Woody.

MURPH: Here we go.

BOB: What do you think makes a good father? You said something earlier about the need to have a good relationship with your kids so I was / wondering …

MURPH: Which you laughed at!

BOB: I was / wondering …

MURPH: Where is your kid— Super Dad?

BOB: … I was wondering what you consider your parental responsibilities to be?

MURPH: Well …

BOB: I mean, how—how often do you have actual contact with your innumerable offspring?

MURPH: May I?

BOB: Go ahead.

MURPH: I see Tom every year at Christmas when he's back in Oz, unless he doesn't come back. I see— Obviously, I see Sally and Oscar whenever I'm in London. When I'm in London I spend lots of time with them.

BOB: How often are you in London?

MURPH: Emma is coming out from Seattle in ah …

BOB: Yes / but—

MURPH: STOP! … She's travelling around with her boyfriend and she's going to come see me in June. It's great—I talk to her regularly on Skype as well. And LuLu is in New Zealand—

BOB: In / summary—

MURPH: Wait! Let me answer the fucking question!!

So, it's mainly Skype. But Marie hates me so that doesn't help and life is … complicated, it's just—

BOB: Yeah, I know all that but what do you think being a father is all about?

MURPH: You're just dying to tell me, aren't you?

BOB: You'd say that you're a good father then?

MURPH: There's worse fathers than me out there.

BOB: Sure / but—

MURPH: There's much MUCH worse fathers—

BOB: Sure. Sure.

MURPH: I talk to all of my kids.

BOB: Yes—

MURPH: Regularly!

BOB: Yes, I know.

MURPH: I know what they're up to.

BOB: I'm just trying to offer you a / sense—

MURPH: I send money to all of them.

BOB: Yeah. I know. I know all that. When you have money, you send money.

MURPH: Well, I can't send it if I don't have it, can I?!

BOB: So, it's about money then? Providing additional, you know, additional income from time to time.

MURPH: Not from 'time to time!' You make it sound like it's—

BOB: You send money regularly then? Like monthly or something?

MURPH: There's not an exact day every month, but I send money, yes. On a monthly. Mostly monthly— Sometimes I send it more often.

BOB: Look I'm not trying to upset you—

MURPH: You've only got one kid!

BOB: But we're not talking about me—

MURPH: Why aren't we talking about you?

Pause.

She wanted more kids. Surely you know that! Surely you can see how / selfish that is—

BOB: Just 'cause someone wants more kids doesn't mean they should have more kids!

> MURPH *waits.* BOB *pours another glass of the black death.*

All I'm saying is that there's a pattern, isn't there? You fall in love and then—you say all this stuff—you make all these plans, blah blah blah and it's all holidays and deep connection and then ... I can tell you what happens next, every time.

MURPH: Why do you talk like that?

BOB: Talk like what?

MURPH: Like I'm your ... student or your ... patient or something.

BOB: I'm trying to be diplomatic, darling.

MURPH: Diplomatic?

BOB: You get so defensive!

MURPH: But that's why I get defensive! Don't you see that?

BOB: Well, surely, that's up to you.

MURPH: You don't let people finish and you ask questions that don't ... When you ask a question, you're really making a statement.

BOB: Don't you think that sounds a bit paranoid?

MURPH: See, what can I say to that?

BOB: I'm just asking you a question—

MURPH: You're making a statement.

BOB: In what way am I making a statement?

MURPH: In that way!

BOB: I just asked you a question.

MURPH: No. No, you didn't.

BOB: Okay, what's a question then?

MURPH: A question is when you want to know the answer.

BOB: So, this is not a question then?

MURPH: No.

BOB: Are you seriously trying to tell me that this is not a question?

MURPH: I'm saying, you already know the answer—so getting the answer is not the purpose of the ... question—the sentence!

> *Pause.*

BOB: And what about this—is this a question?

MURPH: Of course. But it's disguising a statement.

BOB: Okay!

MURPH: Of course, it is, literally, a question—but, getting an answer, is not your intention—you're using it to … transmit an accusation.

BOB: Okay then.

MURPH: It's ah …

BOB: Alright.

MURPH: Ah …

BOB: Fair enough.

MURPH: Trojan horse!

BOB: What am I telling you with this question then?

MURPH: You're saying—

BOB: Go on. Go on.

MURPH: You're saying … You're saying that I'm overly-sensitive and my emotions are ridiculous and hysterical and you're clearly saying that I'm stupid.

BOB: That's amazing! You could be one of those TV clairvoyants!

MURPH: I'm not capable of understanding things the way you do.

BOB: Spot on!

MURPH: So, you twirl everything up into a neat fucking … set of questions that allow you to covertly cast allegations!

BOB: I had no idea I was saying so much!

MURPH: I don't know what you're talking about half the time and there's this tone, you have this tone, this … I don't know. You use it to put yourself outside or above everyone else— It's contempt! That's what it is. Contempt.

BOB: Well, I'm sorry if that's how you feel.

MURPH: Why don't you ever just say what you mean?

BOB: I could say things.

MURPH: Could you?

BOB: Oh, yes.

MURPH: Like what?

BOB: I could say things.

MURPH: Go on then!

BOB: If I wanted to I could.

BOB *pours himself another glass of the black death.*

MURPH: Go on then.

BOB: But it wouldn't be fair.

MURPH: Since when do you care about being fair?

> BOB *drinks it in one and stares at* MURPH *for a moment before speaking.*

BOB: Talking to you …

MURPH: Yes.

BOB: Talking to you is like showing a dog a card trick.

MURPH: … Right. So, what the fuck does that mean?

BOB: Enthusiastic but, you know, baffled.

> *Pause before* MURPH *gets up from the table and goes to the fridge.*

Terrible card players they may be but they are loyal.
I'll give 'em that much.

> MURPH *gets another beer and sits down.* BOB *takes the beer from* MURPH. MURPH *looks at him for a moment before getting another beer for himself.* BOB *keeps talking while this is going on.*

A kind of automatic loyalty—a simpering adoration that comes of such a long history together. Interesting story actually.

MURPH: Goodo.

BOB: A couple of wolves hanging around the campfire, eating scraps and being relatively agreeable. So, we reward them and as a result they prospered through the long winters where their more … disagreeable colleagues went cold. Then these first mutts had pups and we brought the docile ones even closer and we shunned the fierce, independent ones—we chose the ones that gave us the most convincing *impression* of love and loyalty, we bred them with each other until we ended up with an adorable panting disciple—hanging on every word, fine-tuned to provide unwavering endorsement of even the most repugnant human aberrations. Even Hitler could rely on Blondi to look up at him with absolute confidence in his goodness. We distilled a wild animal into a super-sycophant.

MURPH: That's very interesting, Bobby.

BOB: Well, I think so. From wolves to fucking poodles: a most undignified transition. But you see, Murph, it's just not enough, is it?

MURPH: That time already, is it?

BOB: Loyalty is no substitute for intelligence.

MURPH: What was it I did to you?

BOB: I mean, they still eat shit, don't they?

MURPH: He really shouldn't drink—they've all said that.

BOB: Why didn't we breed that out of them, hey?

MURPH: The women, I mean.

BOB: I'll tell you why.

MURPH: 'He changes when he drinks', they'd say.

BOB: Because we like it.

MURPH: You don't need to tell me!

BOB: We like to keep that embarrassing little trait.

MURPH: Something's broken.

BOB: Right there in the mix.

MURPH: Run away!

BOB: Just in case.

MURPH: That's what I'd say.

BOB: They get too big for their boots;

MURPH: And no-one would blame you.

BOB: No matter what they achieve.

MURPH: He's still going at it folks …

BOB: We can always reduce them to shit-eaters!

MURPH: What the fuck are you saying?

BOB: IT'S NOT ABOUT MONEY AND SKYPE!

It's about making the difficult decisions about schools and, and, you know, rules and appropriate punishments and being there to get up in the night and talk them down from nightmares and clean up the shit! It's about trying to go to work on three hours sleep and stay fucking cheery! That's what being a father is!

I worked for the education department for twenty years just for the privilege of staying up all night with Zack when he was sick.

MURPH: And you were a fucking shell—you fucked off in the end!

BOB: In the end! You said it—in the end. I stayed until he was up and away—I held that marriage together until he was—we both did. We hung on like—like fucking … shipwreck survivors! You shoot through before they're out of fucking nappies!

MURPH: You left your fucking family too!

BOB: My marriage failed just like every other baby boomer we know but I didn't go out and start another one! And another one! And another one! I found a way to make sure I could adequately support the one I already had. We're not talking about euthanising the dog in favour of a new puppy here—this is people! Your people! If you can't be there for one, how are you going to raise a trans-continental experiment in genetic diversity!

MURPH: So, we should hang on to the misery then!

BOB: You do what it fucking takes mate!

MURPH: That's a hell of an example to set for your kids.

BOB: I was there!

MURPH: You were physically there.

BOB: Oh please.

MURPH: Have you asked how it was for him?

> *Beat.*

BOB: The point is that you're on the brink of doing it again. You'll flash your jet-setting lifestyle around to impress this child bride of / yours.

MURPH: You can say whatever you like but at least I'm trying. I take an interest in their lives. I like them.

BOB: You're a fucking flake, Murph! You're not a father.

You're a flake and you best admit it now before you get any older. Admit it and repent and hope for the best. Expect the worst and hope for the best, that's what Mum used to say.

MURPH: Great advice from a guy, hiding in South East Asia, plotting the perfect suicide.

> MURPH *heads for the stairs.*

In light of that—you'll forgive me if I step over your advice like a dog turd in the street.

BOB: Where are you going?!

> MURPH *continues up the stairs.*

MURPH: Oh! I gave her your number as well. She took off in such a hurry the other night that she left her jacket and helmets.

> MURPH *disappears up the stairs.* BOB *sits there for a while watching the Bonsai. He gets up suddenly, angrily rummages in the drawers*

looking for a pair of secateurs but instead comes up with a pair of scissors and immediately takes to the Bonsai branch with them. The scissors aren't up to the job. He struggles with it for a while.

BOB: Come on! Fuck ya!

He can't cut through the branch, he bends the branch, trying to bust it off but it won't break. He throws the scissors across the room. He sits back down, defeated. Breathing heavily, he stares at the tree.

3

The next morning. The same Hanoi kitchen.

BOB *is lying on his back in the middle of the kitchen floor.*

His phone rings. He looks around for it but it's on the table. He starts shuffling, on his back, toward the table. When he gets there the phone stops ringing. He settles back into the floor and exhales. The phone rings again. He tries to get up to reach it. He makes it up onto his hands and knees. DUYÊN *appears in the window outside holding her phone to her ear and trying to see inside.* BOB *can't see her. She disappears from view. The phone on the table stops ringing.* BOB *rests there like an old horse hoping not to be ridden. He manages to lay back down on the floor.*

DUYÊN *comes into the house, she still hasn't noticed* BOB *lying on the floor. She is wearing simple white cotton pants and a white top under her shirt. She walks slowly up the stairs, sits down and looks out at the room. After a moment or two of silence she looks down and notices* BOB *on the floor looking up at her. She jumps up and gasps but doesn't say anything. She just stands there with her hands over her mouth. They stare at each other and neither can figure out what to do next.*

BOB: I'm really not sure what one does in a situation like this.

DUYÊN: Neither am I.

BOB: Some sort of shouting and outrage probably but I'm somewhat incapacitated as you can see so why don't we skip all that and go straight to the bit where you try coming up with a viable explanation for creeping around in my house.

DUYÊN: I thought no-one was home.

BOB: I get that. How did you get in?

> He gave you his key, already? He's hopeless!

> *BOB tries to get up but instead crumples to the floor in pain. He shrieks and then lies there groaning. DUYÊN rushes to his aid. She gets down on the floor beside him.*

DUYÊN: Is it your heart?

BOB: No, it's not my heart! Jesus! Sciatica. It's a fucking nightmare.

DUYÊN: Stretch out your leg.

BOB: There's a pinched nerve in my ass sending fire down / my—

DUYÊN: I'm familiar with sciatica! Turn over on your side.

BOB: What for?

DUYÊN: Bring your knee up here.

> *She tries to pull his knee up to his chest to stretch the muscles in his ass.*

BOB: It's those bloody stairs.

DUYÊN: Hold it there.

> *He reluctantly holds his knee toward his chest.*

> Okay. Good. Roll onto your stomach.

BOB: Look, I'll / just—

DUYÊN: And try to relax.

BOB: I'll just take some painkillers.

DUYÊN: Roll over.

BOB: Really, it's okay!

> *He rolls onto his belly. She runs her thumb along the muscle, searching for the source of the spasm.*

> You know what—I'll take some …

> *She finds the spot and gradually applies pressure with her thumb.*

DUYÊN: Ông nằm im coi! (Stop fighting with me!)

BOB: Ối giời ơi! (Holy fucking Jesus!)

> *She puts her body weight into it.*

> What are you doing?!

DUYÊN: Breathe.

BOB: Help!

DUYÊN: Just breathe!

BOB: HELP!

Cries turn to groans, downgrading to panting and deep breathing. She eases up a little.

DUYÊN: How is it now?

Better?

BOB: Fuckenell.

DUYÊN: Yes?

BOB: Yes! Yes …

DUYÊN: Breathe. Keep breathing—

BOB: I am bloody breathing! You'll know if I'm not breathing because I'll turn blue and go limp.

DUYÊN: I released the muscle.

BOB: So, it wasn't a random attack then?

She gradually lets go.

DUYÊN: Stay there for a while.

He adjusts his position.

Don't move, I said!

BOB: My other leg's cramping!

He squirms in agony, holding the other thigh now. She tries to grab his leg.

LEAVE ME ALONE!

Just … please … give me a minute.

DUYÊN: Sorry.

The cramp gradually passes. He lies on his back and relaxes. DUYÊN sits on a chair and watches him.

How is the pain in the other leg?

BOB: It's gone.

DUYÊN: Okay.

BOB: Where did you learn to do that?

DUYÊN: Medical school.

BOB: You're a doctor?

DUYÊN: … Pretty much.

BOB: Well, do let me know when you graduate from 'pretty much' to 'more or less'.

   Beat.

You look younger than you are.

DUYÊN: I suppose that's a good thing?

BOB: Not if you want to be taken seriously.

   He gets up painfully and angrily with one hand on the table and the other outstretched to stop her from helping. She stands up, ready to catch him if he falls.

I'm told you left some items here the other night when you fled the libidinous clutches of Nosferatu.

DUYÊN: You're going to need to let people help you if you don't want to lose your independence.

BOB: Independence! Lose my independence! You can't just say that to people.

DUYÊN: Why not?

BOB: … You can't just spit that out into the room and expect me not to …

DUYÊN: But it's true!

BOB: Look, anyone who doesn't have a few aches and pains at my age hasn't had any fun at all.

   He struggles over to the sink and leans against it.

Independence …

   Pause.

DUYÊN: Not talking about it won't protect you from it.

BOB: From what?

DUYÊN: Specifically? Some cognitive decline—early onset—

BOB: I did Kokoda last year!

DUYÊN: How old are you?

BOB: No diplomatic segue, then?

DUYÊN: About seventy?

BOB: I'm sixty-eight!

DUYÊN: Right. About seventy. You're still pretty young / so I under—

BOB: Thanks very / much!

DUYÊN: You're still pretty young so I can understand your reluctance to face it but that doesn't change the facts.

Beat.

Old Mrs Hương next door was asking me about you.

BOB: Oh yeah.

DUYÊN: She's very worried.

BOB: Is she.

DUYÊN: She seems to think you have no living relatives, which I assume isn't true. I explained to her that Australians … they're not really obligated to their families in the same way. If one family doesn't, sort of, work out, you just start a new one—you move around, disappear, come back. Start again.

Well, it's true, isn't it?

BOB: That explains the little care packages and the mournful looks across the lane.

DUYÊN: She can't figure out why you've been here so long on your own.

Why have you been here so long Bob?

BOB: 'Cause the fucking mangoes are cheap!

BOB *struggles over to the jacket and helmets hanging on the door and gives them to her.* BOB *holds the door open for her.*

If you're looking for a challenge, try slapping some sense into the lascivious larrikin in the Hawaiian shirt. He's got a new family every time I see him.

She starts making her way over to the door.

DUYÊN: I wonder why he puts up with you?

BOB: Easy! I'm one of the very few people who's still willing to put up with him.

She stops in the doorway and turns back to him.

DUYÊN: He's like a … puppy dog and you're / like—

BOB: The big bad wolf? Yes. I know.

Take care out there, won't you? Just—you know—make good choices or you'll end up with a house full of babies and an overdrawn Skype account.

He starts trying to shut the door on her.

DUYÊN: The truth is—!

　　BOB *stops suddenly.*

BOB: The truth! Well, I've always got time for the truth.

　　Pause.

DUYÊN: She's—your landlady—she passed away. Recently … Sorry.
　　The family asked me to make contact with you, the tenant, to see
　　if you're still planning to live here or—

BOB: Yes.

DUYÊN: Oh. Right.

BOB: How did she die?

DUYÊN: Cardiovascular disease. Heart attack.

BOB: I thought heart attacks were reserved for the likes of me, not, you
　　know … how old was she?

DUYÊN: Sixty.

BOB: Sixty. Really? Sixty?

　　BOB *steps back from the door and* DUYÊN *steps back inside.*

Such a lovely—such a good woman. Good women don't have heart
attacks. Do they?

Her husband died not long before I moved in here—she moved
in with her sister's family—but you already know that I suppose.
That's. That's a … That tree belonged to her husband! Look at this.

　　BOB *takes her over to the tree*

His name is on it?

　　He bends over to look at the stamp in the pot. She doesn't look.

DUYÊN: That's his father's name actually.

BOB: I sit here staring at it. She must have stared at it too—She stared
　　at it because he stared at it and I imagine them both staring at it
　　while I'm staring at it and the tree's just being a fucking tree in the,
　　you know, in the room and then there's this branch—this stupid
　　looking branch. I'd have cut it off it weren't for the fact that it looks
　　awfully deliberate—ridiculous! But deliberate.

DUYÊN: It's a sacrifice branch.

　　He looks at her with anticipation, she thinks for a moment.

So … the bigger this branch gets the broader the trunk will become to support it, and the broader the trunk the older the tree looks. And that's the objective.

BOB: Right.

DUYÊN: This whole idea requires a lot of luck though. There's no way to make it happen. I mean, you can't make a branch appear where you want it to but if you're lucky enough to have a bud appear in just the right place, it might turn into a branch and then you can take advantage of the effect it will have on the overall character of the tree.

BOB: But this sacrifice branch comes off at some point?

DUYÊN: It comes off when it has served its purpose.

BOB: You just axe it out and get rid of it when it's no longer needed?

DUYÊN: You carefully remove it so that it heals properly—so it grows over and ultimately, you know …

BOB: No-one will ever know that it existed.

DUYÊN: That's the idea.

BOB: Couldn't you just put it in a nursing home?

Awkward pause.

Food for thought! Always nice to have the young people round to lift ones flagging spirits— Here's your hat—what's your hurry! As me old grandad used to say … and pass my, you know … on to the family— Don't forget your accoutrements!

BOB stands up and turns to the table to get DUYÊN's things. He moves a jumper out of the way, revealing a paperback novel underneath.

Ha! There it is! I've been looking for that.

He sits down and starts flipping through the book.

I got it out for Murph. There's a passage I wanted to ah … let's see here … here we are!

'And so it was, in the half-lit garden, driven by a vanishing memory of spring, he followed the giant footprints down to the lake.' That's—that's not … Why on earth did I underline that?

He continues to look. She realises that he has forgotten what's going on and sits down on the steps to observe and listen.

'The only moment, to settle, deflated and bearable, flew by as if from the window of a train.'

That's not it either.

MURPH materialises in the doorway. He sees DUYÊN *sitting on the stares and before he can speak, she presses her finger against her lips and he stops still. She waves him gently back and he recedes into the space outside the doorway.*

Ah ha!

'Like a vague, dissociative child—humming.
Without irony or fundament grasping,
you hand to me my own voice like a broken toy—
fingers, more useless, never imagined,
right here on the crumbling edge of the ravine.'

He finishes reading the passage, it's not what he was expecting, he looks around.

What the fuck does that mean?

Faintly the sound of the funeral band, which started during his confused oration, starts gaining momentum, clattering along somewhere nearby, getting louder and then lower depending on the direction of the breeze. This will continue throughout the rest of this scene, right through until the burial. He closes his eyes and listens to it before DUYÊN *stands up and re-enters the space.*

I can hear the funeral band.

DUYÊN: It'll be pretty constant for the next couple of days. The tents are set up in the lane, people are going to come and go. The family will eat together day and night and stories will get told—respects paid. Then we take her to the cemetery—just the immediate family.

BOB: Is it true, the music is designed to scare the ghost on to the afterlife?

DUYÊN: I don't know about that.

BOB: If it won't go, it'll haunt the family.

DUYÊN: Maybe.

BOB: What does it say about the afterlife, if it takes a racket like that?

He points to the jacket and helmets on the table in front of him. She moves toward the table.

DUYÊN: Hey Bob?

BOB *looks at her.*

How old are you?

BOB: What do you think?

DUYÊN: Sixty-eight.

BOB: Impressive!

DUYÊN: You look older than you are.

BOB: I shall demand a full refund from my cosmetic surgeon.

DUYÊN: You must have been sixty-seven when you did Kokoda. Whatever that means.

BOB: I did Kokoda last year.

DUYÊN: I know. Because you already told me.

> *She sits down at the table opposite* BOB. *She attempts to make eye contact with him before speaking.*

You know what's going on here, don't you?

BOB: No-one really knows what's going on here—

DUYÊN: You can't afford to waste time hiding—

BOB: Hanoi's a mystery.

DUYÊN: What are you talking about?

BOB: It's … neuronal. That's a good word. You know what that means don't you, Doctor?

DUYÊN: If you keep hiding, you're going to end up lost.

BOB: Confucius?

DUYÊN: Jesus Christ!

BOB: I don't think so. He was all about, you know—don't throw rocks at women / blah blah and—

DUYÊN: Will you stop joking / for a second?

BOB: Hyperbolic metaphors about needles—

DUYÊN: You need to / consider—

BOB: And very, very small camels … no? See, I thought that was pretty / good.

DUYÊN: What about / your son?

BOB: Considering.

DUYÊN: Bob?

BOB: … What about my son?

> *Short pause.*

Look, I appreciate your concern—but there's really nothing wrong with my mind. You must have noticed that my ability to fashion stupendously verbose and socially devastating sentences remains perfectly intact—Murph seems to think I'm making all sorts of allegations in the subtext as well! It's just the rest of me that's falling apart— Look at this. I've broken both wrists, three ribs, left leg—

Points to his left check.

Temporal process—I remember that because it sounds like an anger management course. Most of that was from motorbikes. Discs in my spine are jutting out all over the place like unfinished jenga— Titanium knee! Sciatica. Piriformis, bloody, what's it called.

DUYÊN *gets up and puts on her jacket to leave.*

High blood pressure— Bunions— Cholesterol—

DUYÊN: You need to go home to your family.

BOB: You should see my feet—

DUYÊN: Reunite with your son before it's too late!

BOB: They're like something out of a medical journal.

DUYÊN: Do it for him!

BOB: I AM DOING THIS FOR HIM! Jesus fuck! Do you think I don't want to go back—do you really think I'd be sitting here drinking if I wasn't doing it for him? Fuck sake!

DUYÊN: But that doesn't make any sense.

BOB: Of course, it doesn't—you're twenty-five and childless—you don't understand anything. You're not even a fucking person yet. You're a foetus with a fashion sense!

BOB *smashes a couple of plates in the sink and slumps against the bench from the pain in his leg.* DUYÊN *tries to approach him but he reacts.*

NO!

I refuse to show up after a twenty-year absence and expect him to spoonfeed me and change my nappies.

DUYÊN: Despite all that, I'm sure he still wants to see you.

BOB: I won't put him in that position.

DUYÊN: You don't have the right to decide that for him.

BOB: I won't let him put me in a nursing home.

DUYÊN: How do you know he'll put you in a home?

BOB: Because he's my son! And because he's my son he won't be able to cope and sooner or later he'll do exactly what I did to my parents—then he'll feel bad about that decision for the rest of his life. I will not do that to him or me.

The white Ghosts of Asia aren't meant to come home—that's the whole point of them.

What's in it for you anyway? Why do you care?

DUYÊN *cannot respond. A text message alert sounds.*

MURPH: Fuck!

BOB *looks towards the door.*

BOB: MURPH?!
Is that you?!

Short pause.

MURPH: What?

BOB: What are you doing out there?!

MURPH: … Nothing! Hi Zoo-anne.

DUYÊN: Duyên. Good to see you again Murph.

MURPH *enters trying to act casual.*

BOB: You might have told me you were going to give her your keys.

MURPH: I didn't give her my keys!

DUYÊN: He didn't—I tried to / tell you—

BOB: So how did she get them?

DUYÊN: I've got my own keys. I was just … wanting to grab the stuff I left behind the other night … obviously.

BOB *and* MURPH *are dumbstruck.*

Look, I've gotta go. I'll talk to you later, okay?

DUYÊN *leaves.* BOB *starts putting broken plates in the bin.* MURPH *enters.*

BOB: Why were you lurking back there?

MURPH: What? I wasn't lurking.

BOB: What does she mean she's got her own keys?

MURPH: I'm just as lost as you are.

BOB: She must have got them from the family. To no-one's surprise, privacy is still a developing concept here.

MURPH: Bob. I need to talk to you / about—

BOB: She's got an Australian accent.

MURPH: That's because she lives in Australia— Look I / still—

BOB: I just assumed she had an Australian English teacher.

MURPH: She grew up in Oz—she was born in Hanoi though.

BOB: Did you know she's a doctor? She fixed my back.

MURPH: Does Zack know you're this sick?

BOB: And my landlady is dead.

MURPH: What are you going to do about Zack?!

BOB: She was a kind woman. Helped me out when I first moved in, didn't know much Vietnamese back then.

MURPH: You can't just not mention it to him.

BOB: She gave me the tree.

> *Pause.*

Bob?

Hello!

BOB: I used the word neuronal. I said it right at her. Don't you want to know why?

She asked me why I've been here so long. Then it came to me.

MURPH: What?

BOB: Hanoi is a brain.

MURPH: You told her—Hanoi is a brain.

And how did she take that?

BOB: Are you even listening to me?

MURPH: Bob, I / don't

BOB: Just shut up for a minute!

I know what's going on here—this whole impossible human substrate represents one of the last functioning brains in the ward; still functioning while all around is decay and forgotten purpose … There's a persistent sub-audible hum, a cantering storm of horns and roosters shrieking and right in the middle of it all is a frequency that the entire population is plugged into.

MURPH: Don't do this now, Bob—

BOB: There's something going on here, Murph.

MURPH: Do you understand what she said?
BOB: Listen!

There's eight million people in the city—ninety million in the whole country and if you take a shit in Yên Hòa your granny in Thạch Bàn knows about it before you've had time to flush. But in Australia … in Australia and the rest of the western world people are so irretrievably atomised that achieving anything like this kind of collective consciousness is totally impossible—which is no accident, of course—it's a necessary design feature of consumer capitalism—divide and conquer! Why? So that we will try to spend our way out of it! A grand assembly of grabbing machines! That's what we've become. Deprived of community—reduced to grabbing at stuff to fill the hole—the unfillable hole—until we are stranded neurons—inert and meaningless.

It takes thousands of years of unbroken continuity for a culture to become this tightly woven and only a decade or two to unpick the fabric and kill the entity that it amounts to. The rest of the world is well into terminal decline but not Hanoi—not yet—here the disease is still in its early stages but the concrete has been poured—the synaptic severing has begun—neurons burning out like shorts in the vascular circuitry but for now, Hanoi is alive! The traffic, the ganglions of power lines—the narrow lanes—the chaos! It all adds up to something bigger, Murph!

BOB *leans in towards* MURPH *with conspiratorial zeal.*

Listen to it … I lay here at night listening to it—and from it, a voice, emerges, Murph—from it a soul squirms! A soul that can be felt and heard and loved because the people here are, and have been, in this place since the beginning of time and I'm here immersed in it—briefly absorbed by it and there can be no peace in the heart without surrendering to our place. To our country! To our ground! To the fucking dirt from which we were drawn. And every year the cumquat trees are dug out of the red river flood plain, taken home on the back of motorbikes and placed in the centre of the family table for the two weeks of Tet and the streets smell of citrus blossoms and the traffic is like wind-blown leaves and that hum, that voice speaking just beyond the range of the human ear—dogs in their cages yowl at it while babies learn to walk in the alleyway and the traffic synchronises perfectly with it. I am safe here. I love—I am in love—I have fallen into some abstract but … authentic love with this city. It's unfathomable. It's unstoppable. It's an entity in its own right and I have a strong intuition that this is the reason that Hanoi always wins; if I know nothing else about this place, I know that. These people are constantly underestimated and Hanoi. Always. Wins.

BOB *sits back in his chair.*

Blackout.

4

Next afternoon. Same Hanoi kitchen. The funeral music can be heard in the distance again. The Bonsai is enjoying a spotlight of sun from the window while BOB *sits on a chair facing it smoking a cigarette and drinking coffee. He is totally focused and motionless like the tree.* MURPH *tries to slip into the house and go upstairs without disturbing* BOB.

BOB: Christ! You're at it again.
MURPH: … Sorry. I didn't want to disturb you.
BOB: Okay but don't lurk!
MURPH: I wasn't lurking!
BOB: You were lurking—you're a fucking lurker … put that on your dating profile: 'Geriatric man-child seeks tits and ass for disappointing short-term liaison. Strengths: drunken buffoonery. Weaknesses: a disconcerting propensity for lurking in dark corners.'

This cheers BOB *up no end. He's tidying and giggling to himself.*

MURPH: You're just a straight up fucking arsehole!
BOB: Unfortunate phrasing there, old boy.
MURPH: Fuck mate! You really—I don't need this—I've already had a shit morning, I don't need your shit on top of it.
BOB: Wait!
    Murph!

MURPH *comes back reluctantly.*

I'm sorry, mate.
    Alright old fella. What ticked you off?

MURPH: The bank. You know the one in the old quarter, near the lake.

BOB: The big bank near Hoàn Kiếm?

MURPH: I come in, take a ticket from the machine, wait for my turn. Couple of minutes later, right, this guy in uniform, a staff member, swoops in and starts handing out tickets from a stack he's got in front of him at the desk. He's sitting right there by the door!

BOB: Right.

MURPH: So, we've all taken ours from the ticket machine!

BOB: Right …

MURPH: While he was away having a fucking smoke!

BOB: Okay—settle down soldier.

MURPH: So, I'm sitting over here with this lot, clutching our tickets and waiting to be served and the people who've just come in are getting their tickets from the fella, not the machine, and they start getting called up to the tellers before us, see. So, we're all just sitting there watching this and of course, he's just happily handing out the tickets unaware of all of us who came in while he was off taking a piss.

BOB: Right, so the tickets he's handing out are lower numbers—

MURPH: Exactly.

This woman next to me: she's looking at her ticket and looking around and people are walking in and getting called straight up to the window and she's fucking looking around and looking at me and checking—she keeps checking her ticket and turning it over in her hand. She hasn't figured out that the tickets he's handing out are tickets he pulled out of the machine earlier on, see. She's fucking baffled. And so I go over and try to explain to the guy. I'm saying ya know there's … our tickets—I'm saying, our tickets are wrong and he's trying to give us new ones from this enormous pile and he's putting our tickets in another pile over here, so everyone's on to it now and they're madly exchanging their tickets with the guy, and meanwhile more people are coming in and taking tickets from the … the … fucking machine again. And then those people are going over and sitting where we had just been sitting and they're looking at us in total bewilderment, wondering what's going on and I try to explain to them that they've got the wrong fucking, you know but of course by now it's a loop, a closed loop. They're probably still there now … irretrievable by this point. I just went and found an ATM in the end …

BOB: That's. You see that's … you know— Try getting an experience like that through the travel agent. That's a more authentic Vietnamese experience than going to fucking Ha Long Bay.

DUYÊN *knocks on the door before entering*

DUYÊN: Hi. Can I come in?

BOB: Now she's asking.

MURPH: Allo sweetheart!

BOB: Old mate here just got a true taste of Hanoi.

DUYÊN: Oh. How so?

MURPH: The big bank in the old quarter. What's the point of the bloody ticket machine if—I mean—in Australia or … the machine's there so you don't need the fucking guy to hand them out any more, surely?

BOB: But see this is connected to what I was saying about the overstaffing.

DUYÊN: I / believe

BOB: The machine … sorry. The machine is probably there because someone said: hey we should get one of these machines. So, they just get one. But they still keep the guy. They won't get rid of the guy.

MURPH: Yeah but that's—surely that's …

BOB: Now they've paid a fortune for the fucking ticket dispenser and they're still paying for the guy and they've got themselves a classic Hanoi clusterfuck.

MURPH: That's it!

BOB: They're paying this fella two bucks.

MURPH: Two bucks?

BOB: Yeah.

MURPH: An hour?

DUYÊN: Who told / you …

BOB: Fuck no! Two bucks a day!

MURPH: Bullshit!

BOB: Two bucks a day to grind business to a screaming halt during the lunch time rush.

MURPH: Lucky they're only paying him two bucks a / a day then.

DUYÊN: That ticket guy is the bank owner's nephew.

BOB *and* MURPH *process the information.*

Like, he's exempt from being fired. And he gets paid a shit-ton too. Who told you he only earns two bucks a day?

BOB: Not him in particular then—just, you know, it's well known that the average daily wage is about two bucks. You can't account for familial advantage of course, I know that.

DUYÊN: Speaking of which …

Pause.

BOB: She can't even spit it out!

DUYÊN: … May I use the toilet?

MURPH: It's upstairs to the—

DUYÊN *is off, knowing exactly where it is.*

Left.

Beat.

And why the fuck are there so many KFC places in Hanoi?

BOB: I get the distinct impression the colonel's success has more to do with the beard than his secret recipe. It's almost as if Uncle Ho himself is somehow endorsing it.

Can we really put the connection between a southern white racist and the father of Vietnamese communism down to randomness?

MURPH: So, we did win in the end. All those people got killed trying to stop the advance of communism when we could have just waited fifty years.

BOB: Who could have predicted that a dodgy beard would be the key to cultural colonisation?

MURPH: There's certainly a likeness.

BOB: And these benign things will undo what's left of Communism because in the end, everyone wants their fast food and plastic trinkets.

MURPH: All people really want is freedom.

BOB: Oh, dear sweet Murph.

MURPH: Fuck off!

BOB: They'll never get freedom. They'll never—that's not—it's hard enough to define it, much less actually get it. They will, inevitably settle, for a glittering catalogue of superfluous shit! An endless magnificence of shiny objects to grab at until they are bottomless vessels just like us.

Look at it like that and freedom is just the scenic route back to servitude when all's said and done.

DUYÊN claps loudly as she comes down the stairs. She stands in front of them clapping.

DUYÊN: Bravo!

MURPH: What's she doing?

BOB: Let's have it then.

DUYÊN: I need you to leave, Bob.

MURPH: She says she needs you to leave …

BOB: This again. She thinks I owe it to Zack.

MURPH: Well. Then, I think she's right.

BOB: I'm staying right here.

DUYÊN: No. Seriously. Go back to where you came from.

MURPH: Have I missed something?

DUYÊN: You can fuck off too!

MURPH: What did I do?!

DUYÊN: I dread to think! Go! Both of you! Go home to your families and your expensive fucking mangoes!

Get out of my house!

No-one moves.

MURPH: Is she—you mean … hang on! Hang on!

BOB: She said this is her house.

MURPH: I don't think she meant it literally.

DUYÊN: Vietnam will take you in, as it does everyone, but that doesn't mean you deserve it. Hanoi does not give a shit about you! The people who actually give a shit about you are not here. So, you better fucking run to them before it's too late. Are you hearing me? I'm telling you to fuck off!

No-one moves. Long pause.

BOB: I don't know why you didn't just tell me who you were.

MURPH: Who is she?

BOB: She is the daughter.

Right?

Her mother wanted nothing more than for her to come back to Hanoi when she had completed her studies—that was always the plan, right?

MURPH: Wait. Is this … do you mean the landlady?

DUYÊN: I have decided to move back to Hanoi.

BOB: That would have made her very happy if she had lived to see it.

MURPH: Bob.

BOB: And you want to move back into this house.

DUYÊN: Go to your son.

BOB: The way you didn't go to your mother?

MURPH: Bob!

DUYÊN: You've got dementia.

MURPH: Dementia?

BOB: Nonsense.

DUYÊN: When people know that they are dying they either accept it or they completely deny it.

BOB: I'm not / dying!

MURPH: Is he dying?

BOB: No! Of course not.

DUYÊN: He's got dementia. Lewy body's might explain the mood swings and the confusion. You need to start planning how you're going to manage this.

BOB: Wait a minute—

MURPH: Is it that bad already?

BOB: Wait a minute!

DUYÊN: He's doing what dementia patients do.

MURPH: What's that?

DUYÊN: They play a game that forces you to catch them out.

MURPH: This is serious, Bob!

BOB: No, it's not!

DUYÊN: He's doing it now!

MURPH: Is that what you're doing?

BOB: You both need to calm down. I'm prepared for whatever may come. I've got my dose, remember?

MURPH: Don't start that again. He thinks he's going to kill himself with a syringe full of heroin.

BOB: Morphine.

MURPH: You said heroin to me.

BOB: No, I didn't.

MURPH: Bob. You did. You said you were going to get your son to kill you with dodgy heroin.

BOB: I may be having a couple of memory lapses but this is not one of them— I told you / I had …

DUYÊN: Are you even hearing yourself? Hearing this conversation? Talking about killing yourself rather than allowing your son to see you!

BOB: … She'd been pleading with you.

MURPH: Stop it, Bob!

BOB: To come home.

MURPH: Bob!

BOB: So, you're only here because your mother is dead!

You're no better than us!

MURPH: I'm so sorry Duyên …

BOB: Besides, you don't really want to live here, do you? You're Australian now! We all are—we are three Australians fighting over a country where none of us belong!

DUYÊN: I am not Australian!

BOB: Where were you when your mother needed you most?

MURPH: You always take it too far.

BOB: Oh, shut up, Murph! She's trying to atone for neglecting her own mother, by getting me to go home and die in my son's arms.

MURPH: Bob!

BOB: You're in no position telling me how to have a relationship with my son.

MURPH: Bob, listen!

BOB: Fucking kids, they think it's all about them.

MURPH: BOB!

BOB: WHAT!

MURPH: Zack sent me.

> DUYÊN *spots something on the bench behind them.*

BOB: What?

> *She takes a few soft steps away.*

MURPH: Zack. He said something was up—he said you had withdrawn. He asked me to come visit you and find out what was going on.

> *Pause.*

The rat makes a sudden appearance on the table. MURPH *leaps out of the way.*

The fucking rat is back!

BOB *sees it too. He rushes toward* MURPH.

BOB: Stand your ground or it'll get back through that hole in the wall.

MURPH: What hole in the wall?!

BOB: Don't move!

BOB *picks up an orange and throws it at the rat. The rat runs behind something else.* MURPH *squeals and leaps in the air.*

Stay there, ya big fucking blouse!

MURPH: Well, stop throwing shit at it!

BOB *immediately throws something else at it and again it runs and again.* MURPH *shrieks.*

BOB: I got it! I got it!

MURPH: You're making it angry!

BOB: You're not fucking walking now, are ya!

BOB *scrambles for another projectile while* DUYÊN *composes herself. She takes a strip of white fabric out of her pocket and ties it around her forehead like a head band. She reaches over and picks up a huge meat cleaver from the bench. She wipes tears from her eye with the back of her free hand and launches herself in the direction of* BOB *and the rat.*

MURPH: Bob, look out!

BOB *turns, sees her coming and ducks out of the way. The cleaver comes down with an almighty crash on the table top. The rat screeches. All is still for a moment except for* DUYÊN *panting.*

BOB *slowly gets up.* MURPH *has his hands back in the air now.*

Is it dead?

BOB *leans toward the table to have a look, about to speak.*

BOB: Oh yes.

Blackout.

5

Same kitchen, a few days later. Late afternoon. DUYÊN, BOB *and* MURPH *can be heard arriving at the house together.*

DUYÊN: [*off*] Either way, there's shit in that water—that's what I'm saying!
BOB: [*off*] If there's shit in one lake—there's shit in them all. Same goes for the drains.
DUYÊN: [*off*] Especially down there!

> MURPH *enters the kitchen and goes straight to the fridge. He's wearing one of Bob's nice shirts and ill-fitting jeans he bought locally. Some attempt to spruce himself up has been made because he and Bob have attended Duyên's mother's funeral after being invited by the family.*

> MURPH *grabs three beers, turns to face the doorway and waits for them to enter.*

> DUYÊN *and* BOB *enter.* BOB, *too, is wearing slightly more formal attire and* DUYÊN, *as the immediate family of the deceased, is wearing the traditional white pants and top.*

> MURPH *attempts to hand them both a beer.*

MURPH: Well, that was a beautiful ceremony and I feel very privileged and grateful to have been part of it.

> BOB *waves* MURPH's *offer away.*

BOB: No! No!
MURPH: Cheers!
BOB: Put those away. Since it's a special occasion …

> BOB *approaches the sinister-looking jar with the dirty muslin draped over it.*

MURPH: Oh! Bob, please—not the black death!
BOB: Don't be melodramatic! A significant moment requires a traditional toast.

> BOB *ladles a dram of the black death out into a small ceramic cup and tries to hand it to* MURPH, *who strongly refuses it.*

DUYÊN: Is anyone listening?
MURPH: Yes! Yes—go on.

> BOB, *unperturbed, offers it to* DUYÊN *instead.*

> Bob! Leave it!

> DUYÊN *takes the cup without paying much attention.*

DUYÊN: Last week there was that torrential rain, right?
Right?!

> BOB *is pouring himself a cup now.*

BOB: It's always worse in those lakes and roads south of the old
quarter …
MURPH: Will you shut up!
DUYÊN: You two are a nightmare!
MURPH: Well, I'm listening
DUYÊN: It was full-on—you remember! Proper … fat rain. You know,
the kind of rain that's so fat it makes its own rain when it hits the
ground. So, I'm riding my motorbike along that ah … that main
road—Đường Lê Duẩn, down near the … something lake …
doesn't matter—there's a lot of lakes down there.
MURPH: So many lakes in this town!

> BOB *appears next to* DUYÊN *with his drink raised—*DUYÊN
> *automatically does the same.*

BOB: Up ya bum!
MURPH: Duyên! You don't have to drink that.
DUYÊN: Good pronunciation!

> BOB *knocks it back and* DUYÊN *does the same. Her throat won't
> allow her to swallow and she starts to look panicked. No-one
> breathes. She runs to the sink and spits it out.*

DUYÊN: Oh, God! What did you say this was?
BOB: It's a … traditional rice liquor.
DUYÊN: Someone's fucking with you. That is pure poison. Whatever
you do—don't drink that.
MURPH: Too late! Way too late.

> MURPH *is laughing his ass off.*

DUYÊN: I'm changing my diagnosis. Long-term acute poisoning.

BOB: Cost me a fucking fortune too. Fuck you then! I'll drink it.

Pause.

DUYÊN: Um …

MURPH: Fat rain!

DUYÊN: Right! So, the drains were filling up and overflowing from the rain and suddenly, the water just shot up and I was like—fuck! This is not good. It's halfway up the wheels by now, people are running out of petrol all over the place. It's jamming up fast, and I'm starting to worry about what's in this water. I just figure as long as I'm still going up, I'm okay, but everyone else is doing the same thing— We're pouring in from all directions and I arrive in the middle where I can go no further— Motorbikes as far as the eye can see all face this centre point and we're not going anywhere now! Then the horns stopped—which never happens and we are this … random collection of people facing each other in the rain …

And then, the guy directly in front of me smiles, and I smile back, then we both start laughing, then all the other people around us do the same. I start honking my horn again, but now I'm doing it just for fun, and everyone is laughing and honking— There's a little girl wrapped around the waist of the woman next to me—I reach out my finger and she holds it, drifting in and out of sleep.

It was at least … I don't know—half an hour—before people came in, started figuring it out. Gradually it started to loosen up and disperse.

BOB: Nowhere else but here.

DUYÊN: Nowhere else but here.

It felt like the city was letting me know I was home.

DUYÊN *flops down into her chair, exhausted.*

BOB: I'm sorry about my comment the other night.

DUYÊN: Ha! Which one?

BOB: The whole thing about 'your mother having to die to get you back in the country' thing.

DUYÊN: Yeah, it was a pretty terrible thing to say. But—I mean, you weren't wrong exactly.

Pause.

My mother and I … we weren't great at communicating. We sort of stopped contact once I moved to Australia … Our phone calls were short and infrequent. I soon stopped asking what she's having for dinner, or if there is any gossip at work, how the neighbours were treating her … she didn't really know what was going on in my world either, what subject dilemmas I was having, who I was crushing on, or if I ever missed Dad … as long as I was alive and still at school, I thought that was good enough for her.

And I dreaded going back to Vietnam so much. I knew I would feel like a foreigner if I did, and that's pretty fucking embarrassing. I actually love living in Australia. I mean, the opportunities, the welfare. I didn't want to meet my mum and for her to see how much I've changed. I thought maybe she'd disown me or something. She'd probably lose her mind if she saw my tattoos!

BOB: It's not a lack of love! It's too much. It's too much love if anything. I can tell you she was so proud of you—her daughter the doctor. Don't you imagine for a second that she didn't love you.

This instantly destroys DUYÊN.

Jesus! What's wrong with you, Heff? You look like someone shat in your shoes!

Pause. MURPH *is fuming.*

MURPH: You're really not as smart as you think you are! You know that?

BOB: Right …

MURPH: It shouldn't be this hard! You live, you have kids and, you know, you keep—you just keep fucking going! It's just kids, there's no … it's not a new concept or something!

Beat.

Mate! You've gotta call him. You've just gotta—at the very least, you've gotta tell him what's going on … he's going to ask and I'll tell him but it would be much better if it came from you. I didn't have to be here, you know! I could have just … you know! And then you push and poke and stir the fuckin.

Christ!

BOB: You've really gone above and beyond mate—we can all see that.

MURPH *bites his tongue and squirms a little.*

MURPH: Yeah … yeah. Yeah. You really are a piece of work, Bob! I don't need this shit! I don't care what you do anymore. I'm out of here!

BOB: No, you're not.

MURPH: Yes I am.

BOB: When?

MURPH: Now. Right now!

BOB: No, you won't

MURPH: I will.

BOB: Sweetheart.

MURPH: DON'T FUCKING DO THAT! I've got other people, you know—I've got my kids! I'll put my energy into them!

BOB: You're not going to do that now! Old dogs don't change!

MURPH: You finally got through to me, I guess.

BOB: I can't get through to you! That's the whole basis of our relationship.

MURPH *looks at* DUYÊN.

MURPH: [*to* DUYÊN] Why don't you come with me? We could fly back together.

BOB: Ha! There it is!

DUYÊN: I'm not going back. I've decided to travel around the country a bit.

BOB *is laughing.*

BOB: It was worth one last shot though, wasn't it?

MURPH: [*to* BOB] You are loving this, aren't you?

DUYÊN: Murph! I'm sorry—it's just, I'm a third your age!

BOB: What do you expect?

DUYÊN: If I was forty-three years older … also, this can't come as a shock to you, I mean, what are the odds that you were living in the very house I grew up in? And then I didn't mention it when I brought you home?

The penny finally drops for MURPH.

Right?

I knew, before I landed in Hanoi, that I was going to inherit the house so I came down to have a look at the place. I was sitting on

Mrs Hương's steps when Murph arrived. He was knocking on the door and calling out, then he saw me sitting there and I took off.

MURPH: That was you?

DUYÊN: Then I recognised that fucking shirt of yours in the old quarter and I rescued you from your 'tour guide'.

BOB *laughs again.*

Why don't you book a flight too, Bob?

BOB: I TOLD YOU—I CAN'T GO BACK!

DUYÊN: Statistically you've got somewhere between five and seven years! I wouldn't expect more than two or three of them to be of any use to your family. My advice: go home now and give them everything you've fucking got—every last bit, be courageous. Or, you stay here until your lease runs out and they have to send you home anyway but you'll be of no use to anyone then. You'll just be … freight.

DUYÊN *picks up the Bonsai.*

BOB: [*to* DUYÊN] Where are you going with that?

DUYÊN: It belonged to my grandfather, then my father, and now it's mine. You understand.

BOB: But … but the branch. I mean … I thought we were going to take that branch off.

DUYÊN: Nah, few more seasons—I'll know when it's served its purpose. I thought it was driving you mad anyway.

BOB: Doesn't mean I don't want it.

DUYÊN: I'll be back in a couple of months. Don't be here, Bob. Please don't be here.

DUYÊN *leaves with the tree.*

MURPH: I'm going now too.

BOB: Is that a fact?

MURPH: Yes it is.

Long pause.

What do you want me to tell Zack?

BOB *suddenly remembers something—jumps up and runs to the door.*

BOB: Shit!

MURPH: What is it?

> BOB *runs over to the window and looks out—searching for Duyên.*

BOB: She fucking took it!

MURPH: What?

> *Pause.*

BOB: Nothing.

MURPH: Well …

BOB: Well, what?

MURPH: What should I tell Zack?

BOB: Zack?

> *Pause.*

Oh—my Zack!
What should I what?

> *Pause.* MURPH *turns to leave.*

Murph!

MURPH: What?

> MURPH *puts his hand on* BOB*'s shoulder.*

You'll come up with something.

> MURPH *leaves and* BOB *sits back down on the chair that was facing the Bonsai. He drinks and smokes and watches the space where the tree used to be.*

THE END

RED STITCH | THE ACTORS' THEATRE

presents

Flake

11 OCTOBER – 5 NOVEMBER 2023

Playwright
Dan Lee

Co-Creator
Chi Nguyen

Director
Ella Caldwell

Set and Costume Design
Jacob Battista

Lighting Design
Jason Ng Junjie

Composition and Sound Design
Daniel Nixon

Set Design Associate / Scenic Painter
Khue Nguyen

Dialect Coach
Yuanlei (Nikki) Zhao

Dramaturg
Tom Healey

Stage Manager
Finn McLeish

Assistant Stage Manager
Finleigh Wadsworth

Bob – **Robert Menzies**
Murph – **Joe Petruzzi**
Duyên – **Phoebe Phuoc Nguyen**

This play was developed through Red Stitch's INK writing program.

RED STITCH

THE ACTORS' THEATRE

Artistic Director
Ella Caldwell

Operations Manager
Cecelia Scarthy

Production Manager
David Bowyer

Front-of-House Manager
Penelope Thomson

Finance
Retinue Accounting

Marketing and Development Coordinators
Darcy Kent and David Whiteley

RED STITCH ENSEMBLE

Ella Caldwell
Richard Cawthorne
Jing-Xuan Chan
Jessica Clarke
Kate Cole
Brett Cousins
Ngaire Dawn Fair
Daniel Frederikson
Emily Goddard
Kevin Hofbauer
Justin Hosking
Khisraw Jones-Shukoor
Darcy Kent
Caroline Lee

Chanella Macri
Olga Makeeva
Dion Mills
Georgina Naidu
Christina O'Neill
Joe Petruzzi
Dushan Philips
Tim Potter
Ben Prendergast
Kat Stewart
Sarah Sutherland
Andrea Swifte
David Whiteley
Harvey Zielinski

BOARD

We at Red Stitch acknowledge and pay our respects to Australia's First Peoples and Elders past and present, and offer our gratitude to the Boon Wurrung and Wurundjeri Woi Wurrung peoples of the Kulin Nation, on whose unceded lands we work.

THANK YOU

This development and production of *Flake* would not have been possible without the generous support of our donors and partners

KINDRED DONORS

Jane & Stephen Hains & Portland House Foundation
The Lionel & Yvonne Spencer Trust
Maureen Wheeler AO & Tony Wheeler AO
Lyngala Foundation
Andrew Domasevicius & Aida Tuciute
Carrillo Gantner AC & ZiYin Gantner AC
The James Family Charitable Foundation
Jane Hansen AO
Peter Bartholomew
John Haasz
Graham & Judy Hubbard
Abraham James
Anthony Adair
Michal Alfasi
Beth Brown
Per & Ingrid Carlsen
Simone Clancy
Brian Goddard in Memoriam
The Neff Family
Rosemary Walls
Linda Herd
Michael Kingston
Alex Lewenberg
The Kate & Stephen Shelmerdine Family Foundation
Jane Thompson & Chris Coombs
Christina Turner
Tony Ward & Gail Ryan
Larry Abel
Anita & Graham Anderson

MAJOR PARTNERS

Restart Investment to Sustain and Expand (RISE) Fund – an Australian
Government initiative
Creative Victoria
Cybec Foundation
The Portland House Foundation
Copyright Agency Cultural Fund
Lyngala Foundation
Playking Foundation
Seaborn, Broughton & Walford Foundation
Malcolm Robertson Foundation
The Myer Foundation
Sidney Myer Fund

Rear 2 Chapel Street, St Kilda East, VIC 3183
http://redstitch.net/ | FB: @RedStitchTheatre | T: @redstitch
boxoffice@redstitch.net | 03 9533 8083

WRITER'S NOTE

It seems to me, that the biggest obstacle to writing and just about everything else I try to do, is me. It's a dreadful cliché, I know but this is not some kind of false modesty or insincere attempt at humility, it's a real problem that has made it impossible for me to walk in a straight line. I swing between over-confidence and sudden manic attempts to pull out altogether. All three of these first plays of mine were almost euthanised by me at various points in their development. I'm not kidding. As if infected by a forgotten dream, I wake up one day and decide that it was all an embarrassing mistake and that I needed to make sincere apologies before cutting all ties. Sometimes I went even further, making arrangements to leave town and start a new life in South America or ... Broome! This strategy of, running as far away as I could get, only to discover that I had brought myself with me and there's no out running that, I learnt through years of what alcoholics refer to as 'Geographicals'. It was one such Geographical that got me to Broome in WA where I took advantage of Playwriting Australia's outreach program and started the process of becoming a 'playwright'. After many months of work through the wet season to get a first draft of Bottomless, I rang Steve Rodgers who was mentoring me and broke the sad news, that I wasn't a playwright after all and that I had instead decided to quit my job at Broome Public Library and relocate to Hanoi. Permanently. I had set all this in motion within twenty-four hours of waking up in a panic. Steve said—well, that's a shame because we want to include your play in the National Play Festival in Melbourne this year. Miraculously I started to feel ever so slightly like a playwright again. I'd already bought my ticket and given notice at work but I managed to organise a stopover in Melbourne before I started my new life. Skip forward—skip forward. The festival totally reinvigorates my enthusiasm. The play gets actors assigned to it and we work up a few scenes to present to an audience. It goes very well and I'm a playwright again—a playwright with a slight problem.

Skip forward.

I spend several months, floating around Vietnam and Asia trying to inhabit my new life while feeling rather like an Australian playwright. I get word that an old family friend is living in Hanoi. I move in with him on the outskirts of the city, just north of Ho Tay (West Lake), beside the Red River, opposite the cumquat fields. Skip forward again. Bac Bill, as I called him, was up late one night drinking with an old mate who was visiting from the US. An old mate with a mischievous grin and a Hawaiian shirt. I was woken, as the muffled conversation started to get a little loud and pointed. I came down the stairs toward the kitchen, just enough to hear what they were saying without being seen and because I was a 'playwright' I took a pen and paper with me. I sat on the step and managed to steal three lines verbatim before they went quiet again. One of the lines was "You're a Flake, insert real name! You're going to have children on every continent". I can't remember what the other two lines were but at very least I had a title I liked. Apart from that one line, the play you've just read is fiction. Mostly. Needless to say, eventually I submitted the play to Ella and Red Stitch who have worked on it with me for many years and have talked me down from several attempts to kill it. I am endlessly grateful that they kept it alive and I want to thank everyone who has helped develop this story to its completion. Without you and your generosity it really would never have happened. I also want to give special thanks to Chi Nguyen for helping me build the character of Duyen. I knew I wanted Duyen to exist in the play but it was Chi who made her real—gave her depth and authenticity. My immense gratitude goes to Ella and Tom Healey for making this story work, along with the incredible cast who have stuck with this story for many years.

Dan Lee

DAN LEE
PLAYWRIGHT

Dan has written three plays. *Grey Nomad* was produced in LA by the Australian Theatre Company in 2017. *Bottomless* was produced by 45 downstairs in Melbourne in 2018, and *Flake,* which was developed by Red Stitch Actors Theatre—INK writer's program between 2016 and 2023. The first two productions were directed by Iain Sinclair. *Bottomless* was the last play to receive the RE Ross trust script development award and went through further development at Melbourne Theatre Company for a Cybec-staged reading. Dan worked on several new play ideas with the help of the Besen family funding at Malthouse theatre in Melbourne at some point. It was a long time ago. There are more plays coming.

CHI NGUYEN
CO-CREATOR

Chi is Vietnamese artist based in Melbourne, and a graduate of The Victorian College of the Arts (VCA) where she received the Grace Marion Wilson Scholarship for Excellence in Acting. Chi's recent TV credits are recurring role Megan Vu in Amazon Prime's original series *Class of '07*, Jeanette Dao in Amazon Prime's original series *The Wilds*, and Juliana in ABC's *Fisk*—a comedy series in which Chi performed and co-wrote two episodes with Kitty Flanagan. She also played Au Pair in Victoria Thane's web series *Sonia and Cherry*, and starred in the first ever Vietnamese-Australian comedy web series P*hi and Me*, which she is currently co-writing Season 2 for under Screen Victoria's support. In 2022, Chi's performance as Mum/Amber in Melbourne Theatre Company's *Laurinda* was nominated for Outstanding Performance by the Green Room Awards. In 2019, Chi wrote and performed a season of her debut solo comedy cabaret *Lotus* (Nominated Best Cabaret at Melbourne Fringe

2019). Other theatrical credits include Tam in *The Shift Theatre's Hallowed Ground: Women Doctors In War* (toured with Regional Arts Victoria and internationally to Edinburgh Fringe 2019), Lead Player in Arena Theatre Company's *Air Race* and Mother Courage in VCA's *Mother Courage and Her Children*.

ELLA CALDWELL
DIRECTOR

Ella is a theatre director and actor. She grew up on the far south coast of N.S.W, later studying Creative Arts at the University of Melbourne. A founding member of Red Stitch Actors' Theatre, Ella has been Artistic Director of the company since July 2013. During this time Ella has steered the company's new writing program, INK, and established PLAYlist, a biennial site-specific festival of music and new writing. Most recently, Ella directed the world premiere season of *Monument* by Emily Sheehan, also developed through the INK program. Previous directorial work includes the Australian premiere seasons of Ella Hickson's *Oil* and Annie Baker's *The Antipodes*, and the world premiere of Caleb Lewis' *The Honeybees*. Ella also co-directed the sold out Victorian premiere season of Joanna Murray-Smith's *Fury* and the Australian premiere production of *Incognito* by Nick Payne. During 2020 Ella directed Watching, an audio play for eighteen actors written by Vidya Rajan and Morgan Rose, commissioned by Red Stitch. As an actor, Ella recently featured in Morgan Rose's *Fast Food* and *desert, 6:29pm*, both directed by Bridget Balodis. *desert, 6:29pm* went on to a sold out season at Wuzhen Theatre Festival in China on the company's first international tour. Previous acting credits include *The Realistic Joneses* by Will Eno, *The Village Bike* by Penelope Skinner, *Love, Love, Love* by Mike Bartlett, *Midsummer—A Play with Songs* by David Greig and Gordon McIntyre, *Oh Well Never Mind Bye* by Stephen Lally, *The Laramie Project—10 Years Later* by Moises Kaufman, *Stop.Rewind* by Melissa Bubnic, *The Winterling* by Jez Butterworth, *Crestfall* by Mark O'Rowe, *Outlying Islands* by David Greig, *The Night Season* by Rebecca Lenkiewicz and Bug by Tracy Letts.

JACOB BATTISTA
SET AND COSTUME DESIGN

Jacob Battista is a Melbourne-based theatre designer and practitioner. Jacob completed a Bachelor of Production at the Victorian College of the Arts. Some of his design credits include *Admissions* (Melbourne Theatre Company); *A Simple Act of Kindness, Grace, Iphigenia in Splott, Love, Love, Love, Jumpers for Goalposts, Belleville* and *Out Of The Water* (Red Stitch); *Hand to God, You're a Good Man Charlie Brown* and *Bad Jews* (Vass Theatre Group); *Rust and Bone* (La Mama Theatre); *Burn This* (fortyfivedownstairs); *Songs for a New World* (Blue Saint); *MEMBER* (Fairly Lucid); *Frankie and Johnny in the Clair De Lune* (Collette Mann/ fortyfivedownstairs); *The Lonely Wolf* (Dirty Pretty Theatre/MTC Neon); *Therese Raquin* (Dirty Pretty Theatre); *Carrie The Musical* (Ghost Light); and as associate set designer *Bernhardt/ Hamlet*, and *Shakespeare in Love* (Melbourne Theatre Company). Jacob was a recipient of a 2016 Besen Family Scholarship at Malthouse Theatre working with Marg Horwell on *Edward II* and is also a recipient of an Australia Council ArtStart Grant. Jacobbattista.com.au

JASON NG JUNJIE
LIGHTING DESIGN

Jason is a multifaceted theatre maker with a wide spectrum of experience, working on shows that range from international arts festivals to non-profit youth productions, often simultaneously. His portfolio benefits from his critical eye for semiotics, creative energy for problem-solving, and passion for collaborating with other artists. His dynamism and drive, coupled with his background as a teacher, have brought him opportunities in multiple roles, from production and stage management, to lighting and set design, as well as mentoring and consulting. He graduated from the Theatre Studies Programme at the National University of Singapore in 2006. After spending time in events management and education, Jason returned to theatre in 2013. He moved to Perth in 2017 where he studied Lighting at WAAPA, before moving to Melbourne in 2020. Australian credits include *Jiangshi* and *Cephalopod* with Squid Vicious, *Bad Baby Jean* with The Last Great Hunt, *Coming Out* with Lucy Holz, *Lenore* with The Knack Theatre, and *Dear Mama* with Wit Incorporated. Outside theatre, Jason is currently training to be a veterinary nurse.

DANIEL NIXON
SOUND DESIGN

Daniel is a composer, sound designer and multi instrumentalist. He has performed with the Melbourne Symphony Orchestra, Orchestra Victoria, John Farnham, Yothu Yindi, Sebine Meyer, Mikko Frank and many others. He has written and recorded multiple albums and worked extensively as a session player, programmer and producer. He has scored and designed numerous films, plays and dance works, including work with Flashgun Films, Cascade Films, Little Ones Theatre, A Daylight Connection, Red Stitch Actors Theatre, American Girl, Universal Television,

Disney Pictures, Al Jazeera, The National Gallery Australia, Melbourne Theatre Company, Queensland Theatre, Malthouse Theatre, Chunky Move, Dirty Pretty Theatre, Griffin Theatre Company, Ensemble Theatre, Madman Entertainment, NBCU, ABC, Netflix, Arts House, HBO, Films by Jove and many others. In 2020 he won the Greenroom award for Malthouse Theatre's Production of Loaded.

KHUE NGUYEN
SET DESIGN ASSOCIATE / SCENIC PAINTER

Khue Nguyen is a Melbourne based artist represented by Art Atrium Gallery, Sydney. Khue has exhibited internationally in Malaysia and Vietnam. Khue holds a Master Degree in Visual Arts with over 40 years experience working in the arts industry across Fine Arts, Graphic Design, Installation Arts, Public Arts, and Performing Arts. Flake is Khue's first involvement with theatrical set design. In 2010, Khue Nguyen was the first Vietnamese Australian to reach the finals of the Archibald Portrait Prize. Since arriving to Australia in 1988, Khue has had two solo exhibitions, participated in thirty-six group exhibitions, won sixteen prizes in Fine Arts, nine prizes in Graphic Design, and received four Arts Grants. Khue created three public artworks for the Little Saigon Business Precinct including the Saigon Welcome Arch (in collaboration with Maribyrnong City Council, Group GSA and McBride Charles Ryan Architects). Khue is currently working on the *Springvale Boulevard Project*—an urban design development in Springvale in collaboration with Hassell Architects commissioned by the City of Greater Dandenong. Khue's passion for performing arts and dance led him to complete his *Master with Body Language Through the Medium of Dance* series of work.

YUANLEI (NIKKI) ZHAO
DIALECT COACH

Yuanlei (Nikki) Zhao is a voice and dialect coach based in Naarm/Melbourne. Originally from Shanghai, Nikki is a bilingual coach, Lessac practitioner, a recipient of the Creative Victoria's Creative Learning Partnerships grant and is a tutor at VCA. Nikki has worked as dialect coach on productions including: for Creative Learning Victoria: *Abbotsford DNA Through Time*; for NIDA: *When Vampires Shop*; Goldilocks; for Red Stitch: *Caught*; for Griffin Theatre: *Sex Magick* and for SBS: *Appetite*.

TOM HEALEY
DRAMATURG

Tom graduated from the Victorian College of the Arts in 1989. Over the last thirty years he has worked as a director, a dramaturg and an actor for theatre companies around the nation. His previous productions include: *American Song*—national tour, *Jumpers for Goalposts* and *The Shape of Things*—national tour (Red Stitch Actors' Theatre); *Heisenberg* (MTC); *The Kid* (Griffin); *The Spook* (Malthouse Theatre); *Elegy, The Sign of the Seahorse, Ancient Enmity, Insouciance, The Fat Boy* and *Falling Petals* (Playbox); *Let's Get it On* (Room 8); *Doris Day—So Much More Than the Girl Next Door* (Boldjack); *Disarming Rosetta* and *Inside Out* (Hothouse Theatre); *Good Evening* (Token) with Sean Micallef and Stephen Curry; *The Man In Black* (Folsom Prison Productions); Eddie Perfect's solo shows, *Drink Pepsi, Bitch* (Malthouse Theatre and tour); and *Angry Eddie* (Chapel Off Chapel). Tom is currently the Associate Dramaturg at Red Stitch. Previous positions include Head of Acting and Directing at Flinders Drama Centre, Literary Manager at the Australian Script Centre, Artistic Director of the Australian National Playwrights' Conference and Artistic Associate at Playbox. He has been a proud member of the MEAA since 1989.

FINN MCLEISH
STAGE MANAGER

Finn is an emerging theatre manager and performer based in Naarm/Melbourne. She is currently studying Psychology at Monash University. Recent production credits include: Assistant Stage Manager; *Far Away* (Patalog Theatre), *Crocodile* (Spinning Plates Co.), *Julius Caesar* (Melbourne Shakespeare Company); Co-Production Manager; *Shakespeare in Love* (Monash Uni Student Theatre), and Assistant Director; *Marie Antoinette* (Monash Uni Student Theatre). Recent performance credits include *Jack in Into the Woods* (Monash Uni Student Theatre) and *Elmire—Tartuffe* (Monash Uni Student Theatre).

FINLEIGH WADSWORTH
ASSISTANT STAGE MANAGER

Finleigh is an all-round theatre professional with a passion for creative expression. He has dabbled in many roles within Theatre Production from management to lighting and sound, and relishes his time spent performing on stage too. Finleigh is someone who enjoys experiencing the Arts, not just working in them. He brings a strong level of care and respect to every production he is a part of, and you're about to feel the effect that has!

JOE PETRUZZI
MURPH

Joe graduated from the National Institute of Dramatic Art (NIDA) in 1984 and from 1988–1990 furthered his training in New York at HB Studios. He has worked extensively in television and film both in Australia and overseas. Television credits include *The Devil's Playground* (TV Series) as well as ongoing roles in *Stingers*, *Possession*, and *The Violent Earth*. Joe has featured in *Bordertown* and *The Last Resort* (for the

ABC), as well as appearances in *Rush, Neighbours, McLeod's Daughters, Salem's Lot, Blue Heelers, Beastmaster, Crash Palace, White Collar Blue, Water Rats, Police Rescue, On the Beach, All Saints, The Magistrate, Fields of Fire, Mafia Marriage,* and *Flipper*. Joe's film work includes *Love's Brother, Paws, The Real Macaw, Mambo Kings, Dingo, Citizen Cohn* and *Captain Johnno*. In 2017, Joe was invited to join the Red Stitch Actors' Ensemble after being involved in *Jurassica* (2015) and *The Village Bike* (2016). Since then, he has performed in *The Way Things Work* (2017), *American Song* (2017), *desert 6.29pm* (2017), *Right Now* (2018) and *Fury* (2018). Most recently Joe has been involved in *Prayer Machine* (2021) and *A Simple Act Of Kindness* (2022) both developed through the Red Stitch INK program for local writers.

ROBERT MENZIES
BOB

Robert Menzies' (he/him) theatre credits include *Cosi* for Melbourne Theatre Company / Sydney Theatre Company; *A Midsummer Night's Dream, Macbeth, The War of the Roses, Julius Caesar,* Seneca's *Oedipus, The Golden Age,* and many others for Sydney Theatre Company; *Macbeth, Hamlet, The Weir, The Cherry Orchard, Music, Queen Lear* and *August: Osage County* for Melbourne Theatre Company; *Measure for Measure, The End, Ghosts* for Belvoir; *The Government Inspector* for Malthouse Theatre. Television credits include *Glitch, Jack Irish,* and *The Beautiful Lie*. Robert's film credits include *Cactus, Canopy, Home, Siam Sunset, Three Dollars, Lamb, Bliss* and *Heatwave*. Robert has received five Helpmann Award nominations, winning in 2005 for *The Plague Year*. Robert has also been nominated for three AFI Awards and three Green Room Awards, winning for performances in *The End* and *The Selection*.

PHOEBE PHUOC NGUYEN
DUYÊN

Theatre includes: *Miss Saigon-Wrong* (script reading, 2021), *Legally Blonde* (Waterdale Theatre Inc., 2023) Film/Television includes: *Beauty, Rich & Rare* (short, 2023). Phoebe was born and raised in Saigon, Vietnam and moved to Australia in 2017. She is a freelance singer and pianist. She was classically trained in piano at the Ho Chi Minh City Conservatory of Music (2001-2011) and has most recently trained in acting at the Howard Fine Acting Studio (2022). This is Phoebe's debut with Red Stitch.

RED STITCH ACTORS' THEATRE

Red Stitch is a creative hub, offering scope for artists to make work they are passionate about in a sector where such opportunities are limited. As the ensemble and executives of Red Stitch, we provide a platform where leading practitioners can hone their craft and take risks, and emerging artists can work alongside mid-career and seasoned professionals. We play a vital role in the development and presentation of new Australian works through our INK playwriting program, promoting local voices alongside acclaimed contemporary international work which may not otherwise be seen by local audiences.

www.redstitch.net

Red Stitch would like to thank the following supporters who generously contribute to our INK program.

CREATIVE VICTORIA

Australian Government
RISE Fund

MALCOLM ROBERTSON FOUNDATION

THE PORTLAND HOUSE FOUNDATION

CITY OF PORT PHILLIP

Cybec Foundation

THE ROBERT SALZER FOUNDATION

S,B&W Foundation
SEABORN, BROUGHTON & WALFORD FOUNDATION
Supporting the Performing Arts

PLAYKING FOUNDATION

Lyngala Foundation

COPYRIGHT AGENCY
CULTURAL FUND

SIDNEY MYER FUND

Kindred

THE MYER FOUNDATION